A Guide to SITE and ENVIRONMENTAL PLANNING

A Guide to SITE and

JOHN WILEY & SONS, INC.

ENVIRONMENTAL PLANNING

HARVEY M. RUBENSTEIN

New York | London | Sydney | Toronto

Library of Congress Catalog Card Number: 68-26851
SBN 471 74440 9
Printed in the United States of America

To my wife Toby, without whom . . . .

Preface

Both creative ability and imagination are essential to site and environmental planning. It is my purpose in *A Guide to Site and Environmental Planning* to present an approach to design based on factual information so that creative talent may be used to its utmost advantage. This book has evolved out of the need for a reference text that combines a design approach with the background of technical information necessary for design development. By providing sufficient technical data I have tried also to keep the tedious task of searching for information in other references to a minimum.

Chapters follow phases in the development of a site plan and include material explaining site selection and analysis, land use and circulation, visual design factors and natural elements in site organization, contours, grading and earthwork calculations, site drainage, alignment of horizontal and vertical curves, and details in the landscape.

Students and practicing professionals in architecture, landscape architecture, civil engineering, city and regional planning, and environmental design will find this book useful for varying scales and types of project in site planning work. Numerous diagrams, sample problems, and photographs of actual projects are of particular value as visual supplements.

This book has developed from research for my site planning courses in the School of Architecture and Urban Design of the University of Kansas, but many ideas discussed here were generated by the landscape architecture departments of Pennsylvania State University and the Harvard Graduate School of Design.

Harvey M. Rubenstein

Lawrence, Kansas
December, 1968

Contents

A Guide to SITE and ENVIRONMENTAL PLANNING

FIG. 1-1. Unity of building and site is attained by reinforcing landform with architecture. Marin County Civic Center, San Rafael, Calif.

1 Introduction

Site planning is the art and science of arranging the uses of portions of
land. The site planner designates these uses in detail by selecting and
analyzing a site, forming a land-use plan, organizing vehicular and pedestrian circulation, developing a visual form and materials concept, re-
adjusting the existing landform by design grading, providing proper
drainage, and finally developing the construction details necessary to
carry out the project. Although he may determine the over-all uses of a
site, this is not always the case. The planner, however, does arrange for
the accommodation of the activities the client has specified. He must relate these components to each other, to the site, and to structures and
activities on adjacent sites, for, whether the site is large or small, it
must be viewed as part of the total environment. Site planning is profes-
sionally exercised by landscape architects, architects, planners, and
engineers. (See Fig. 1-2.)

CRITICAL THINKING PROCESS

In site planning, as in other forms of problem solving, the critical think-
ing process of research, analysis, and synthesis makes a major contribu-
tion to the formation of design decisions. Research material may be
gathered from existing projects, books, photographs, or experiments. The
designer must formulate his program and list the elements required to
develop the project. Being open-minded is essential to creativity. The site
planner must constantly strive to ward off preconceived thoughts or influences which might close his mind to worthwhile ideas. First intuitive

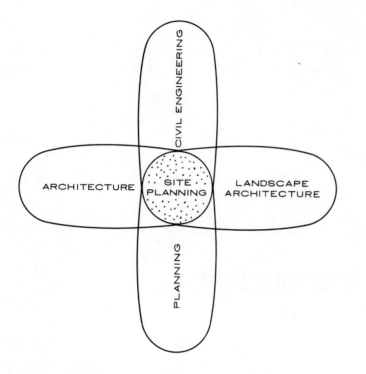

CIVIL ENGINEERING

ARCHITECTURE

SITE PLANNING

LANDSCAPE ARCHITECTURE

PLANNING

thoughts should be recorded and shown graphically whenever possible since they are often pertinent to the development of the program.

Analysis of the site should consider all existing features, both natural and man-made, in order to determine those inherent qualities that give a site its "personality." A topographical analysis of its existing features is mandatory. Emphasis should be placed on the site's relationship to the total environment and its special values or potentials.

FIG. 1-2. Practicing site planners.

Sample Student Problem: A Community Center

Program
1. Pedestrian and vehicular access.
2. Parking—10 visitors, 10 staff, 100 members.
3. Softball field and touch football field.
4. Two tennis courts and basketball court.
5. Tot-lot and bike parking.
6. Crafts area.
7. Truck service.

Site Factors
1. The character of the site is steep and open, except where foliage is dense and there are large existing boulders.
2. The site is essentially split in half by foliage and steep slopes.
3. It has northeast exposure—cold, but good for winter sports. Most of it is well protected from wind.
4. Soil condition is glacial till with large boulders at depths averaging eight feet, except where exposed in woods.

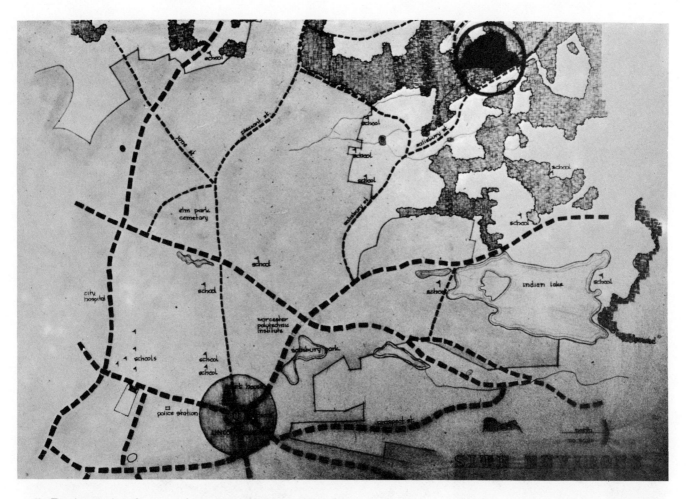

FIG. 1-3. **FIG. 1-3.** Site environs: the community center is emphasized by the circle at the upper right. Salisbury St. is the primary route to the site.

5. Drainage is adequate from stream upward (west).
6. The first 250 feet fronting on Salisbury Street is very low and wet.
7. Views expand as elevation increases.
8. The pond is a very important feature.
9. The pines to the north are very dense and attractive.
10. Except for the northwest and southeast boundaries, the site is entirely surrounded by single-family residential development.
11. Public water and sewage lines run along Salisbury Street.
12. The strongest entry is from Salisbury Street; second strongest from Moreland Street; the third from entry to Temple Sinai; and the fourth from the residential road to the west. (See Figs. 1-3 and 1-4.)

Synthesis, based on a land use plan, evolves out of the analytical phase. The land use plan is developed from abstract relational diagrams that are rearranged by warping, shifting, stretching, or rotating them to adapt to physical conditions; they are not arbitrary. Therefore test as many alternatives as possible and list negative and positive points in order to choose the best diagram. The design synthesis will be an interpretation and articulation of factors into a design that fits the site without seriously altering functional relationships. (See Figs. 1-5 and 1-6.)

Within the image: SITE ANALYSIS

FIG. 1-4. Site analysis: The natural, cultural, and aesthetic factors of the site are graphically illustrated and the two possible building sites are numbered.

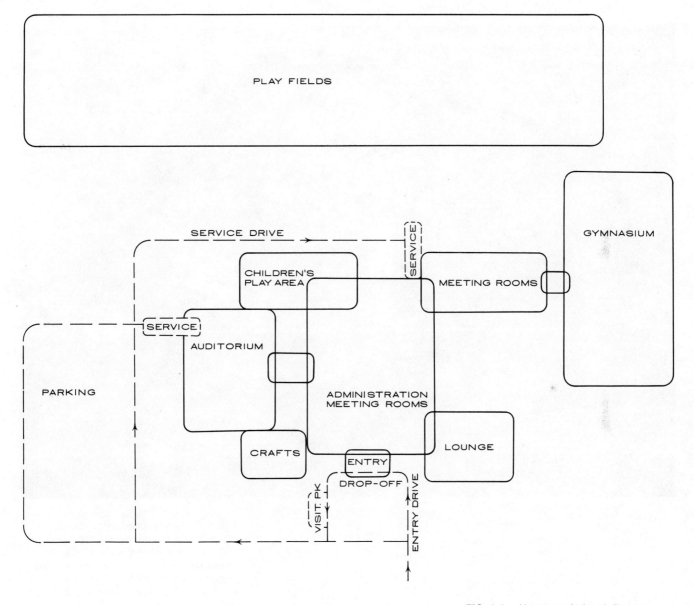

FIG. 1-5. Abstract relational diagram.

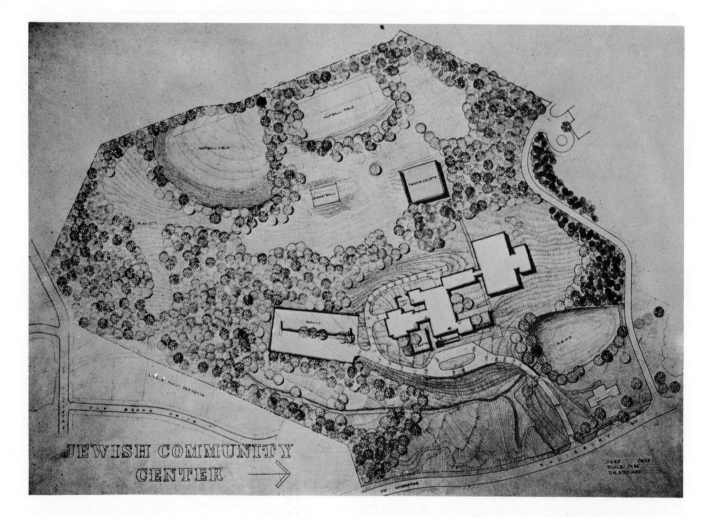

FIG. 1-6. Design development: building site one was chosen for development. In this location harmony is established between the community center and the existing landform on the site. There are good views of the building from Salisbury Street and the entry drive adapts well to topography. People approaching the building have a choice of using the drop-off area or driving directly to parking facilities.

FIG. 2-1. Nature within the urban fabric of the city: Central Park, New York City.

2 Site Selection and Analysis

Site investigation made concurrently with the formulation of program objectives ensures the flexibility of the site's potential and the integration of its natural and cultural features with the design. In order to develop the best possible site for accommodating project objectives, a program must be carefully prepared. Because it develops from specific needs, these needs determine the over-all objectives.

Program development is based on the study of factors such as site requirements and sizes, types of building and site construction, and the uses of materials. The program is in a constant process of refinement as these factors are studied. The completely developed program will include a schedule of required facilities, their times of completion, and their priority for construction.

In the first of two methods of establishing a site alternative sites are considered within a general location and a choice is made of the one that best meets the preliminary objectives. This is a good approach to design. In the second method the site location is chosen by a client before the establishment of a program or even before a use for the site has been determined. An inappropriate site or factors of cost may lead to a forced site solution, a solution that often creates problems which need not otherwise exist; for example, excessive grading due to a forced solution may raise the estimated construction costs of a project, thereby compromising other program requirements, and it may well destroy the natural site features that could have been the primary reason for choosing the location.

On large projects such as campus planning, shopping centers, parks, or planned community developments site selection may require a detailed analysis of potential sites. The following method is a useful aid not only in selecting a site but also in analyzing one that has already been chosen. The analysis of the site and its environs includes all natural, cultural, and aesthetic factors that affect it. These features influence final site selection and provide clues to site personality that will be helpful in establishing guidelines for later development.

Any information that is inventoried should be illustrated graphically. On these illustrations important factors may be abstracted, or isolated and emphasized, to build a firm foundation from which to interrelate all known elements. With basic objectives in mind, the site planner may use each of the items in the following list of natural, cultural, and aesthetic factors, where they are applicable, for site selection or for the development of a given site. The flexibility of detail with which these items are investigated and the order in which they are studied depend on the complexity of the project and whether the items are used for site selection or analysis.

Natural Factors

1. Geologic base and landforms.
2. Topography—topographic maps, slope analysis.
3. Hydrography—streams, lakes, swamps, bogs, and watershed drainage.
4. Soils—classification of types and uses.
5. Vegetation.
6. Wildlife.
7. Climatic factors—solar orientation, summer and winter winds, precipitation, and humidity.

Cultural Factors

1. Existing land use—ownership of adjacent property, and off-site nuisances.
2. Linkages.
3. Traffic and transit—vehicular and pedestrian circulation on or adjacent to site.
4. Density and floor area ratio.
5. Utilities—sanitary and storm systems, water, gas, and electric.
6. Existing buildings.
7. Historic factors—historic buildings or landmarks.

Aesthetic Factors

1. Natural features.
2. Spatial pattern—views, spaces, and sequences.

NATURAL FACTORS

Geology

Which geologic processes have affected the site, its formation, and the type of rock below the surface of the soil? At what depth is the rock located? Type and depth of rock present many questions of its adequacy as a base for the foundation of some buildings, but test borings taken at several locations on the site will provide the answers. These borings should be located and plotted on the topographic map. The site planner may consult with a geologist to facilitate interpretation of the borings or to consider any problems that may occur concerning the geologic base and its relevance to the project. (See Fig. 2-2.)

By the use of aerial photographs viewed stereoscopically geologic and physical features become distinguishable to the educated eye and patterns influencing future land use may evolve. If not trained in aerial photo interpretation the site planner may find the geologist helpful here too.

Landforms. Irregularities of the earth's surface are known as landforms. Knowledge of their kinds and characteristics will influence design if the site is part of, or encompasses, such an irregularity. Landforms are derived from volcanic, glacial, or erosional processes. They should be examined for their origin, topography, drainage, vegetation, and—when photographed for aerial identity and characteristics—tone. We will examine the characteristics of alluvial fans as an example. Alluvial fans occur, particularly in mountainous areas, where a stream discharges onto a plain or valley floor. The result is the formation of a fan-shaped landform. The fan shape varies in proportion to the size of the watershed.

FIG. 2-2. Geologic base: the depth and type of rock below the soil's surface, is a most significant factor in site development.

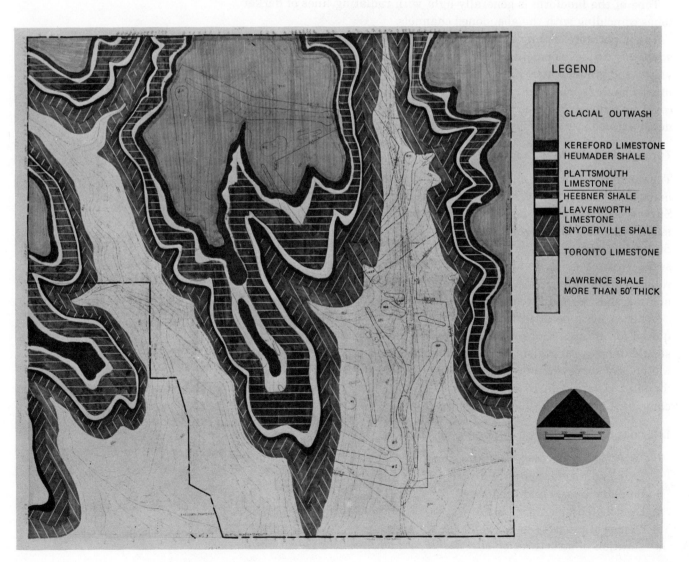

LEGEND

GLACIAL OUTWASH

KEREFORD LIMESTONE
HEUMADER SHALE

PLATTSMOUTH
LIMESTONE
HEEBNER SHALE
LEAVENWORTH
LIMESTONE
SNYDERVILLE SHALE

TORONTO LIMESTONE

LAWRENCE SHALE
MORE THAN 50' THICK

It develops as one or more divisions of the main stream channel deposit coarse sediments in the channel and the slope decreases. As the channel becomes choked and overflows, it builds up in elevation until the stream finds another location in a lower portion of the fan. This process is repeated until a symmetrical fan is formed over 90 degrees or more.

The surfaces slope smoothly in all directions from the apex of the fan, which is the origin of the stream from the mountain. Slopes vary in relation to the texture of materials. They are relatively flat wherever fine materials are deposited. In fans formed from coarse materials the surface is marked with distributary channels. Alluvial fans may vary from a radius of several inches to several miles.

Young alluvial fans usually do not contain a surface drainage system, but older fans that have ceased to grow may have some surface runoff as floods overflow the parent stream. During periods of low water virtually all flow filters into the alluvial fan near the apex and moves as groundwater to the edge of the landform.

Vegetative cover in arid areas is principally grass with a few scattered trees. At the edge of the landform, heavier vegetation may be evident if seepage water is present. Being heavier in association with distributary channels, vegetation in humid areas may cover the entire alluvial fan.

Tone of the landform is generally light with radiating lines of darker tones coinciding with the abandoned channels.

The importance of alluvial fans is based on their being well drained and adaptable to development of all types. They have good air drainage, views, and groundwater. In times of storm, however, the unstable distributary channels may shift, thereby eroding a new channel or completely covering a developed area with a new layer of debris brought down by a newly formed system of distributaries. (See Fig. 2-3.)

Topographic Surveys

The analysis of a site and its environs presupposes that topographic maps have been obtained. These maps, available from the U. S. Geological Survey, show locations and elevations of natural as well as man-made features, relief, and vegetation. They cover most areas of the United States at a scale of 1:24,000 or 1 in. = 2000 ft. They come in the 7.5 minute series, with a 10 ft. contour interval. Specific characteristics such as relief, hydrography, roads, buildings, and features such as bogs, swamps, and marshes are indicated.

When a more detailed topographic map, such as 1 in. = 40 ft., is required for an area that has not already been surveyed, the site planner should employ a registered surveyor to obtain the necessary data. Methods of surveying may differ; however, aerial surveys are often used for sites covering large areas such as city or state parks, university campuses, or housing subdivisions. (See Fig. 2-4.)

Information Required on Topographic Maps

1. Title, location, owner's name, engineer, certification, and date.
2. True and magnetic north, scale.
3. Property lines, building lines.
4. Existing easements, rights of way on or adjacent to site.
5. Names of property owners on adjacent sites.
6. Location of structures on site, basement and first-floor elevations of

FIG. 2-3. Alluvial fan abstracted in model form.

FIG. 2-4. Aerial photography aids in obtaining an over-all view of the site.

buildings, as well as walls, curbs, steps, ramps, tree wells, drives, and parking lots.

7. Location and sizes of storm and sewage systems; manhole, catch basin, and curb inlet drains with rim and invert elevations.
8. Outline of wooded areas, location, elevation on ground, and type and size of trees with 3—4 in. trunk caliper or larger.
9. Hydrographic features—rivers, lakes, streams, swamps.
10. Location of telephone poles, light standards, fire hydrants.
11. Rock outcrops or other outstanding site features.
12. Road elevations at intervals of 50 ft.
13. Grid system of elevations at intervals of 50 ft.
14. Contour interval—1, 2, or 5 ft.

Slope Analysis

A slope analysis aids in recognizing areas on the site that lend themselves to building locations, roads, parking, or play areas. It may also show if construction is feasible. A parking lot, for example, should have a grade of under 5%. If there is no land available which meets this requirement, regrading will be necessary. The cost of grading may determine if the development of a site is feasible.

A typical breakdown of grades would be 0—5, 5—8, 8—10, 10—15, 15—20, 20—25, and 25+. These grades are established by measuring the distance between contours at a given scale and contour interval. The formula is $D = \dfrac{\text{contour interval}}{\% \text{ grade}} \times 100$, where D is the distance between contours at a particular grade to be set. In order to set a 5% grade at a contour interval of 2 ft. the equation would be

$$D = \frac{\text{contour interval} \times 100}{\% \text{ grade}}$$

$$D = \frac{2 \text{ ft.} \times 100}{5\%}$$

$$D = 40 \text{ ft.}$$

The over-all pattern of slopes will emerge through slope analysis, which helps the site planner determine the best land uses for various portions of the site, along with feasibility of construction. (See Fig. 2-5.)

Hydrography

The drainage patterns on a site may greatly influence a design. All water bodies, rivers, streams, and drainage channels must be traced diagrammatically in order to be assayed and used advantageously. Hydrographic features have a bearing on relating activities to the land, and

FIG. 2-5. Slope analysis.

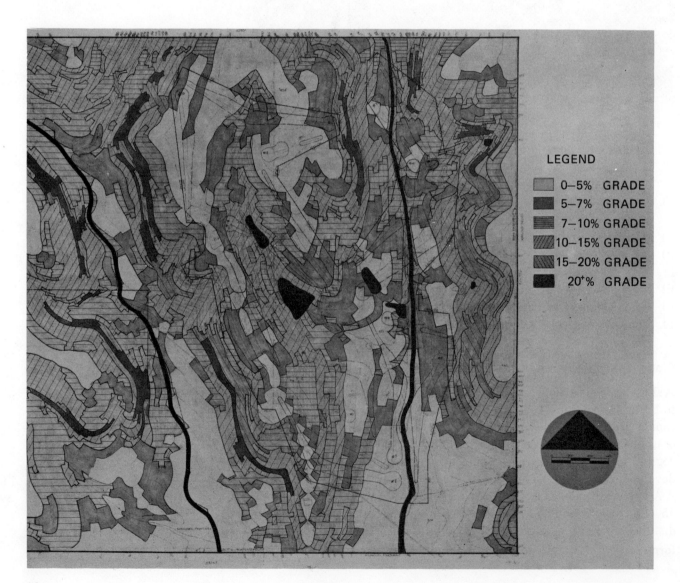

LEGEND

- 0–5% GRADE
- 5–7% GRADE
- 7–10% GRADE
- 10–15% GRADE
- 15–20% GRADE
- 20⁺% GRADE

they are of primary importance in developing a system for site drainage that makes use of existing watershed drainage patterns. Streams and lot lines, for example, should be placed adjacent to each other in a subdivision, so that the site planner does not divide the lot unnecessarily. (See Fig. 2-6.)

Soils

What is the land capability classification of soil on the site (its most suitable use while protecting against erosion)? Will it support vegetation or are there limitations which reduce choice of plants? Is the soil alkaline, neutral, or acidic? Tests of soil profiles by agronomists will give the answers.

Consider the characteristics of the site, both surface and subsurface. At what depth is the water table located? Test pits may be studied to observe the infiltration or passage of water into the soil surface. Runoff occurs when precipitation exceeds infiltration of water into the soil.

FIG. 2-6. Drainage patterns.

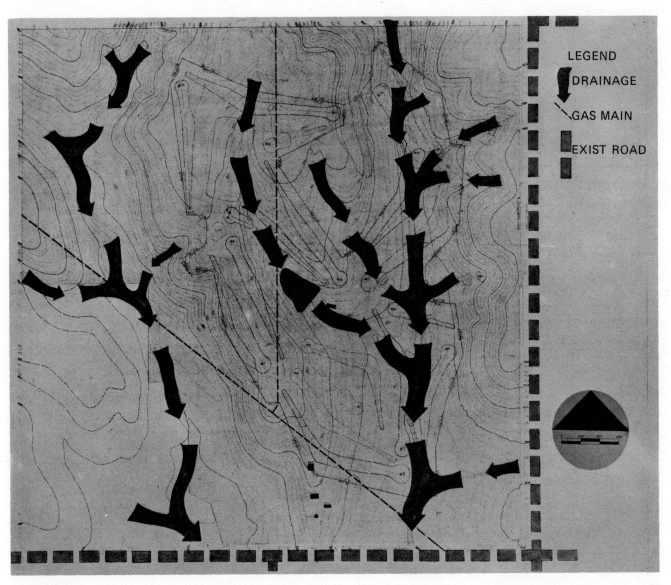

LEGEND

DRAINAGE

GAS MAIN

EXIST ROAD

Drainage patterns on the site, therefore, may best be traced while it is raining.

The depth of water table is most important. If it is too close to the surface 6 ft.$^{\pm}$, there will be adverse effects on a building basement and the project cost will rise as increased waterproofing, pumping, and the use of pilings become necessary. If the water table is too low, problems concerning water supply and cost may occur.

In areas where septic tanks are to be used in conjunction with residential development, the ability of soils to absorb and degrade sewage effluent quickly must be studied. If the soil is not suited for this use, problems such as water pollution and the smell of raw sewage will occur.

Vegetation

By taking cognizance of vegetation on a site before development, one may make use of large existing trees rather than neglecting them and later being forced to purchase small ones which will take many years to attain maturity. Note the name, size, and location of large existing trees 3 – 4 in. or more in caliper. Observe their form, branch structure, foliage color, and texture. If a site is heavily wooded, a carefully planned thinning of the trees may open potential vistas.

Review the ecology of the surrounding area to find which trees or shrubs are native and which varieties may be added for wind protection, shade, buffer zones, screens, or backdrops. Having previously reviewed soil characteristics, the analyst should also research which, if any, nutrients must be added for improved plant growth. (See Fig. 2-7.)

Wildlife

Wildlife is an important consideration, especially when choosing sites for park or recreation areas. Since fishing and hunting are major recreational activities, choosing land for these uses depends upon wildlife as a natural resource.

Wildlife also adds color, form, and movement to the landscape. Existing wooded areas inhabited by wildlife may be preserved as park land in conjunction with residential subdivisions.

Climatic Factors

Elevation difference, character of topography, vegetative cover, and water bodies influence the climate, which in turn affects the site. Climatic data available from the U. S. Weather Bureau includes temperature, precipitation, wind, humidity, and amount of sunshine.

For each 300 ft. rise in height from the earth's surface, temperature decreases approximately 1° F in the summer. Certain cities (Brazilia, for example) are located at higher altitudes in the otherwise hot climate of the tropics. Differing height in topography also affects microclimate; cool air flows toward low points or valleys at night, but higher side slopes remain warmer.

Precipitation and temperature are the two major factors affecting vegetation, although wind, humidity, and soil characteristics are also important influences.

In cool and temperate climates vegetation may be used to block winter winds. Sometimes trees have adjusted to being part of a forest area and,

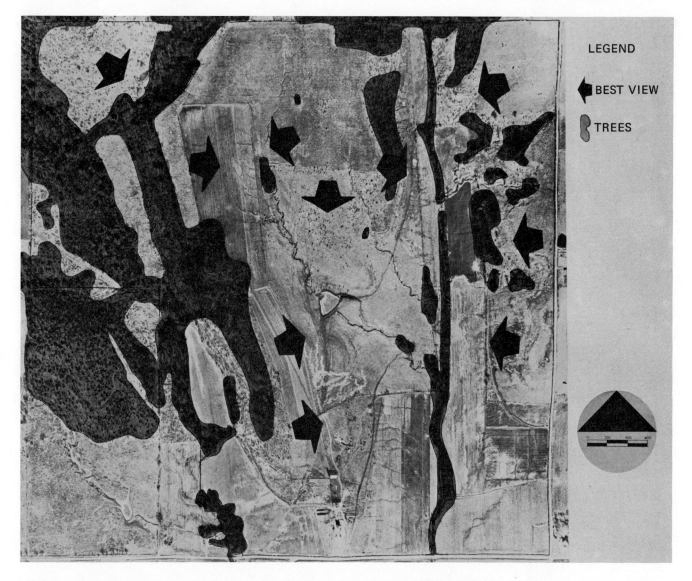

LEGEND

◀ BEST VIEW

❨ TREES

FIG. 2-7. Vegetation: the location and identification of vegetation on a site helps to preserve and take advantage of native plant material.

if left to stand alone as a single element, may die because of strong winter winds. Wooded areas can also be opened or thinned to allow sunlight pockets for residential or other developments in cool climates. Deciduous trees are used to provide shade and may alter microclimate several degrees in summer.

Water bodies also influence the climate of the site. Oceans and large lakes retain their heat in winter months as land masses cool and they are cool in summer as land masses warm. The water bodies adjacent to land, therefore, moderate temperature. This influence decreases with distance inland from the water body.

Climates can be divided into four general types—cool, temperate, hot arid, and hot humid. In each of these climatic zones the site planner should investigate the solar orientation for buildings, the best facing slopes, and the part of the slope that makes use of air flow for warmth in cool climates or for breezes in temperate or hot climates.

Figures 2-8 to 2-11 represent factors for each climatic zone; residences are placed to receive the best solar orientation for each climatic region. (See Figs. 2-12 to 2-14.)

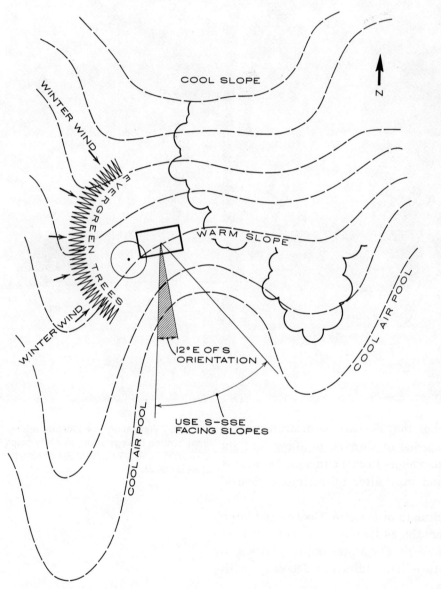

COOL SLOPE

N

WINTER WIND

EVERGREEN TREES

WINTER WIND

WARM SLOPE

COOL AIR POOL

COOL AIR POOL

12° E OF S
ORIENTATION

USE S–SSE
FACING SLOPES

FIG. 2-8. Cool climates.

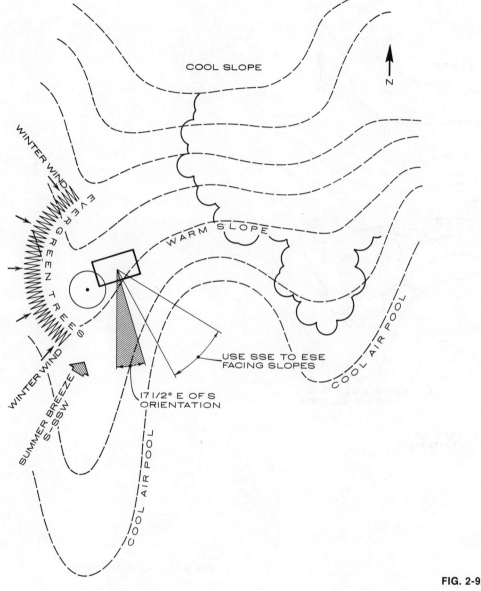

FIG. 2-9. Temperate climates.

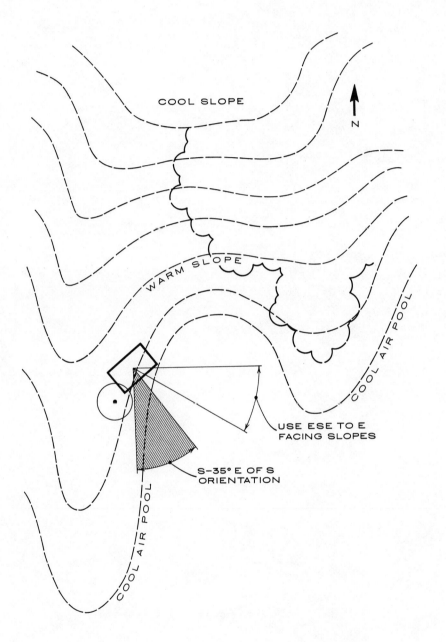

COOL SLOPE

N

WARM SLOPE

COOL AIR POOL

USE ESE TO E
FACING SLOPES

S—35° E OF S
ORIENTATION

COOL AIR POOL

FIG. 2-10. Hot arid climates.

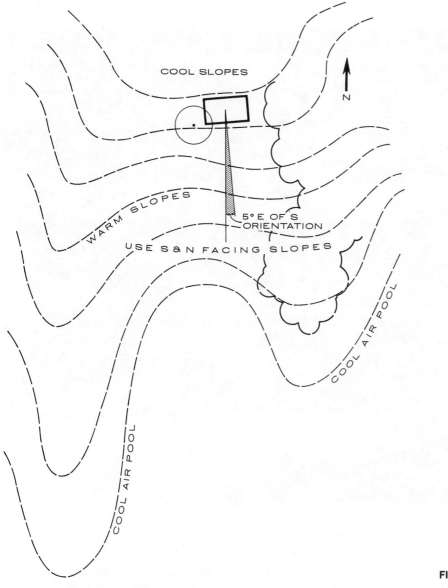

FIG. 2-11. Hot humid climates.

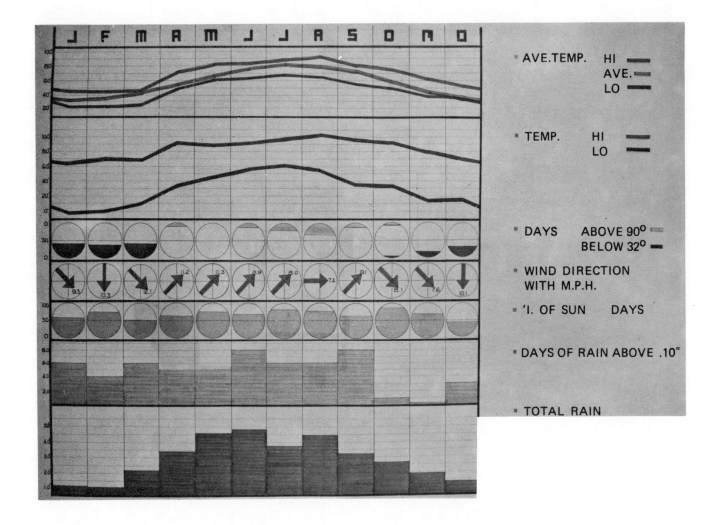

FIG. 2-12. Climatic data: information from the weather bureau can be illustrated in charts or graphs for easy interpretation.

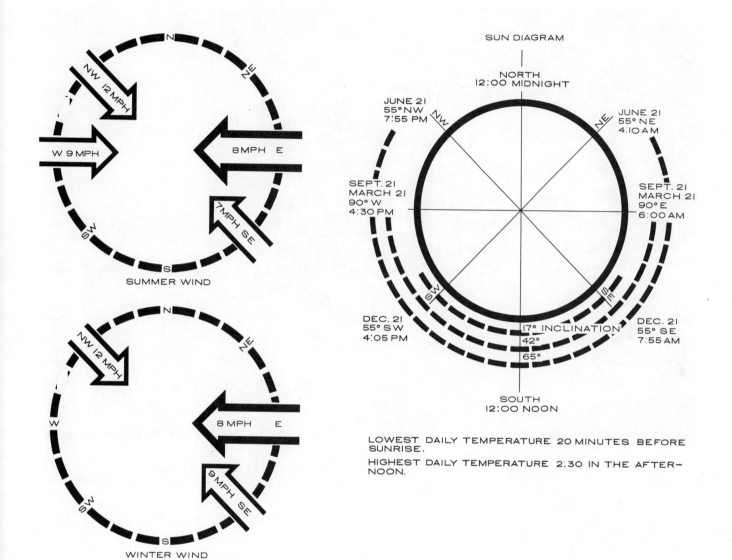

SUN DIAGRAM

NORTH
12:00 MIDNIGHT

JUNE 21
55° NW
7:55 PM

JUNE 21
55° NE
4:10 AM

SEPT. 21
MARCH 21
90° W
4:30 PM

SEPT. 21
MARCH 21
90° E
6:00 AM

DEC. 21
55° SW
4:05 PM

17° INCLINATION
42°
65°

DEC. 21
55° SE
7:55 AM

SOUTH
12:00 NOON

SUMMER WIND

WINTER WIND

LOWEST DAILY TEMPERATURE 20 MINUTES BEFORE SUNRISE.

HIGHEST DAILY TEMPERATURE 2:30 IN THE AFTERNOON.

FIG. 2-13. Wind and sun diagrams: Vancouver, Canada.

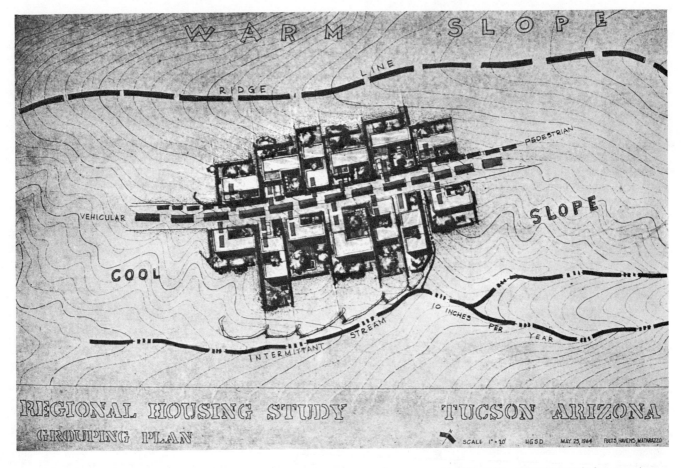

FIG. 2-14. A typical study for grouping housing: the hot arid climate of Tucson, Ariz.

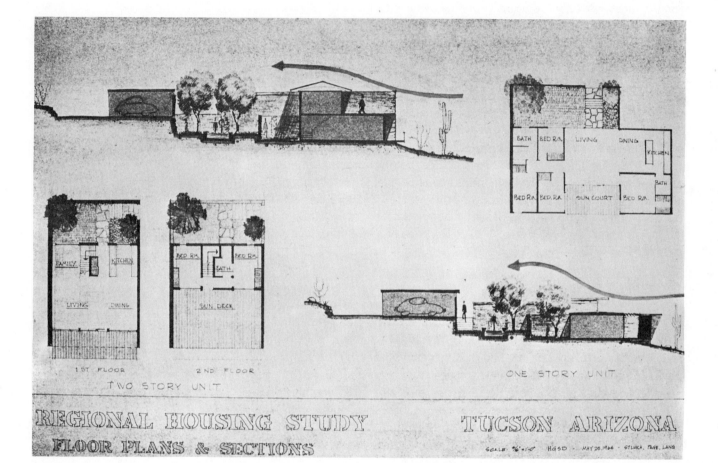

REGIONAL HOUSING STUDY   TUCSON ARIZONA

FLOOR PLANS & SECTIONS

CULTURAL FACTORS

Existing Land Use

The pattern of existing land use must be designated in relation to the site. Community facilities both public and semipublic, residential, commercial, industrial, and recreational are inventoried to denote over-all trends in development which may have bearing on uses of land adjacent to and including the site under study. (See Figs. 2-15 and 2-16.)

In conjunction with the study of existing land use, the site planner should meet with the adjacent property owners to find out, if possible, what future development of their sites may be under consideration and whether this development will be in conflict with uses planned on the new site.

Off-Site Nuisances. Off-site nuisances, whether visual, auditory, or olfactory, and safety hazards must be investigated. If one or more of these problems is uncontrollable, an alternative site may have to be chosen. Among visually disruptive elements are power lines, water towers, certain industrial complexes, highways, billboards, and junkyards. Possible auditory nuisances include heavy automobile, rail, or air traffic, or noise made by large numbers of people. Olfactory nuisances originate in dumps or in chemical and other wastes. Safety hazards result from the lack of linkages in areas of heavy traffic. Severe and sudden changes in land, such as a steep cliff at the edge of a site, may be a safety hazard.

Linkages

In the process of studying the location of the site and its relation to adjacent properties and to the community, all existing ties or linkages, if any, should be specified. Linkages may involve the movement of people, goods, communication, or amenities. Now ask whether, by the addition of parkways, parks, or pedestrian overpasses or underpasses, these linkages need strengthening? Community facilities such as nearby shopping centers, employment hubs, residential areas, churches, schools, parks, and playgrounds should be inventoried in relation to the site. Determine whether adequate linkages exist, and, if not, decide how they can be established or improved by future development.

Traffic and Transit

What is the relationship of traffic patterns to each other and to the site? Are there adequate roads in the vicinity? If the site is urban, does public transportation service the area? Depending on the complexity of the problem, automobile, bus, railroad, and air circulation should be reviewed to show if, and how, these facilities will integrate with future site development. (See Fig. 2-17.) Graphically plot transportation systems and their location or routes when they are available. Check the volume of traffic or frequency of flights to determine whether additional routes are necessary.

Density and Zoning

Density is an important sociological and legal element in most types of development. In residential development, it is expressed in numbers of

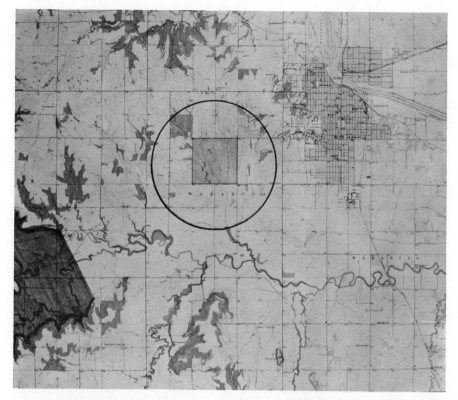

FIG. 2-15. Site location: a site should be located in relation to the larger environment. The site encircled in the photograph above is an area of a proposed planned unit development in Lawrence, Kansas.

FIG. 2-16. Existing land use.

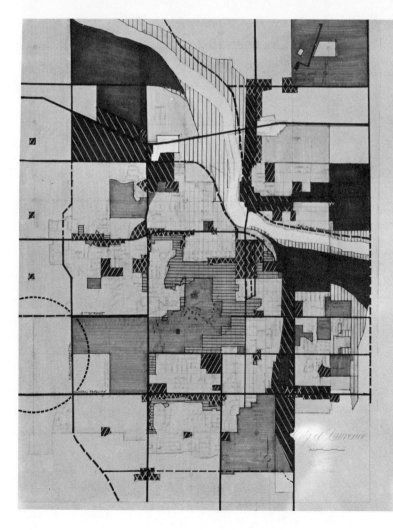

LEGEND
☐ LOW DENSITY RESIDENCE
▤ MULTIPLE FAMILY RESIDENCE
▧ COMMERCIAL
▦ PARKS, PUBLIC & SEMI-PUBLIC
▨ SCHOOLS
▥ STORM DRAINAGE
▨ LIGHT INDUSTRY
▰ HEAVY INDUSTRY
▬ MAIN ROADS
▬▬ PROPOSED MAIN ROADS

families or dwelling units per acre. Density may also be used to express floor area ratio or gross floor area covering the site—if all floors were spread out and assumed to be one story in height as compared with total site acreage. (See Fig. 2-18.)

Cities have zoning regulations concerning standards of density because of economic, social, and functional implications. Density may influence privacy, freedom of movement, or social contact among people. Zoning regulations, easements, codes, and mineral rights must be checked before a site is developed in order to work within these regulations or to determine if changes would be desirable when possible. Information concerning zoning and much of the other information on codes, regulations, and names of property owners is available at city hall. (See Fig. 2-19.)

FIG. 2-17. Existing and proposed road pattern.

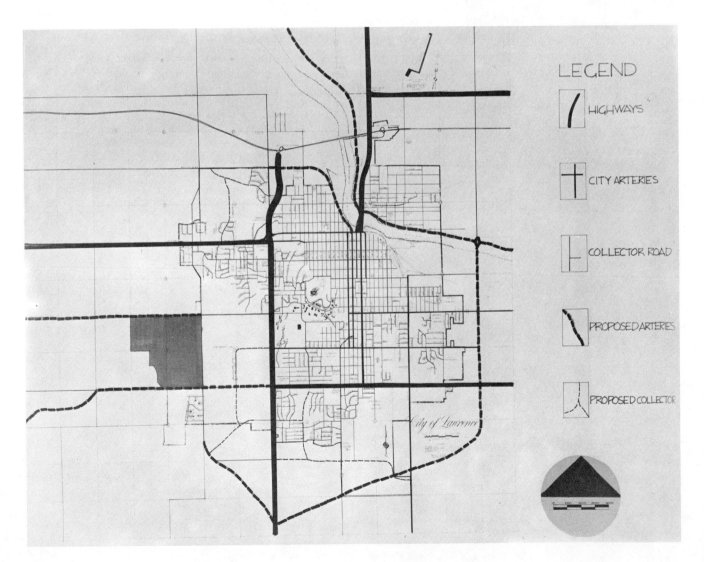

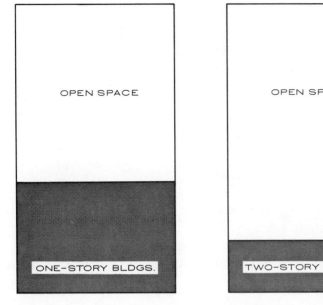

OPEN SPACE

ONE-STORY BLDGS.

OPEN SPACE

TWO-STORY BLDGS.

FIG. 2-18. Floor area ratio.

FIG. 2-19. Zoning.

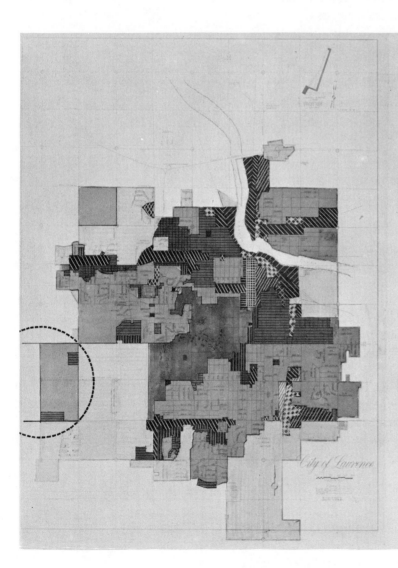

City of Lawrence

LEGEND

RESIDENTIAL

- RS1 SINGLE FAMILY
- RS2 SINGLE FAMILY
- RM 1 MULTIPLE FAMILY
- RM 2 MULTIPLE FAMILY
- RM 3 MULTIPLE FAMILY
- RD RESIDENCE-DORMITORY
- RO RESIDENCE-OFFICE

COMMERCIAL

- C1 OFF-STREET PARKING
- C2 NEIGHBORHOOD
- C3 CENTRAL
- C4 GENERAL
- C 5 LIMITED

FLOOD PLAIN

- FP FLOOD PLAIN

INDUSTRIAL

- M 1 LIMITED
- M 2 GENERAL
- M 3 INTENSIVE

Utilities

All utilities should be located on the site and shown graphically for consideration in site development. All utility lines should be in open areas or under streets for easy maintenance. Water is the most critical utility for growth at the community level and may have to be piped in from outside areas. Other utilities such as electricity, gas, or telephone usually present fewer problems. (See Fig. 2-20.)

Existing Buildings

If a project is to be expanded buildings on the site must be shown graphically and their uses and facilities studied. Size, floor area, and existing conditions must be inventoried. Existing buildings will strongly influence the physical layout of the new site plan and will help to establish the grading and drainage pattern on the site. They also may determine the choice of future architectural expression in building type, color, and materials in order to insure coherence and unity in design.

History

A campus plan or other large project may have a meaningful background that influences future expansion. It is then pertinent to ask, "Will historic factors be of consequence to the project?" The history of these projects should be investigated and shown graphically so that relevant influences may be considered in the design phase. The investigation may show, for example, that specific buildings should be preserved within the redevelopment of a campus, as should other historic buildings or landmarks in other projects. (See Fig. 2-21.)

AESTHETIC FACTORS

Sites on which future development is planned must be analyzed to determine significant aesthetic factors. Natural features and spatial patterns are all important in relating design elements.

The character of many sites is distinguished by the arrangement of these elements. This is true, for instance, in the following examples of sites that have a unique character in the midst of an industrial area of Pittsburgh, or within an urban residential area in San Francisco. (See Figs. 2-22 and 2-23.)

Natural Features

Sites may be endowed with outstanding natural features of earth, rock, water, or plant material. Landforms, rock outcrops, ledges, boulders, lakes, streams, bogs, or wooded areas have scenic value and may be incorporated along with architecture in site development. One of these features, for aesthetic value alone, may be sufficient reason for designating an individual site for construction. The designer must use them to advantage, rather than reducing their impact through improper site treatment. (See Figs. 2-24 and 2-25.)

Spatial Pattern

Views. Views on a site may be pleasing or objectionable. They may bear heavily on the orientation of a building and therefore should be carefully studied. An outstanding view must be handled properly to be preserved

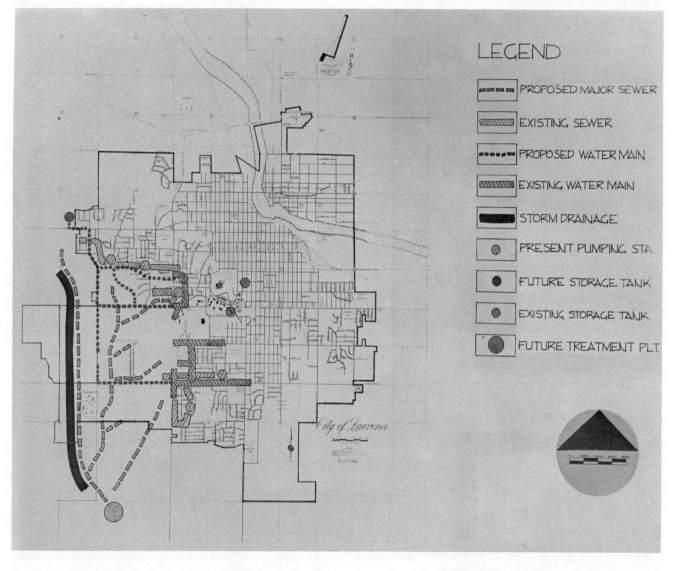

FIG. 2-20. Utilities.

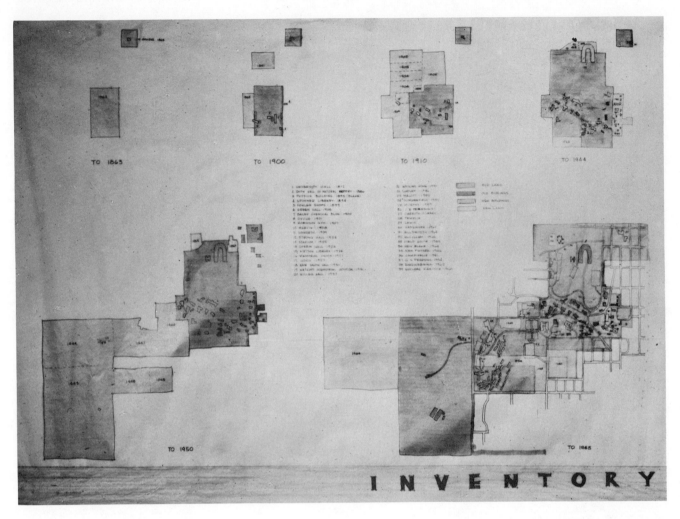

INVENTORY

FIG. 2-21. History: the historic growth of Kansas University since 1865 may influence its future development.

FIG. 2-22. Industrial character of Pittsburgh, Pa.

or accentuated. Views are framed, open, enclosed, filtered, or screened. Be sure to note their sequence. Do they seem static or do they, as if by mystery, attract attention and draw movement toward them? A view should be completely revealed only from its best vantage point, not given away at first glimpse. An observer can be made to anticipate a view and then see it from its best location for its fullest impact. When studying views on sloping sites, the site planner should also consider the angle of vertical view.

FIG. 2-23. Residential character of San Francisco, California.

FIG. 2-24. Natural rock outcrop.

FIG. 2-25. Bog.

Views on a site must also be compatible with proposed activities and their relation to each other because nuisances both on or off the site may disrupt them. In many cases it is possible to use vegetation, fences, or walls to screen objectionable visual, auditory, or olfactory elements. Billboards, power lines, junkyards, or parking lots, for example, may be handled so that they present no visual problem. Power lines may be placed underground, and junkyards and large parking lots may be depressed below grade level.

Vistas. A vista may be a natural or completely man-made view. It has a dominant focal point or terminus that is strongly emphasized and is enframed and balanced by minor elements which form masses to enclose the vista and screen out conflicting objects from its composition. The open space or line of sight of the vista is a strongly directional element leading the observer toward the focal point for closer observation. (See Figs. 2-26 to 2-31.)

FIG. 2-26. A framed view from the walk approaching a dormitory complex at the University of Colorado, Boulder.

FIG. 2-27. A filtered view through trees.

FIG. 2-28. The line of sight to the Charles River is a strong directional feature at Harvard Married Student Housing, Cambridge, Mass.

FIG. 2-29. An open view from the overlook area at Grand Canyon National Park.

FIG. 2-30. An open view from Cypress Point, which overlooks the Pacific Ocean at Carmel, Calif.

FIG. 2-31. A vista.

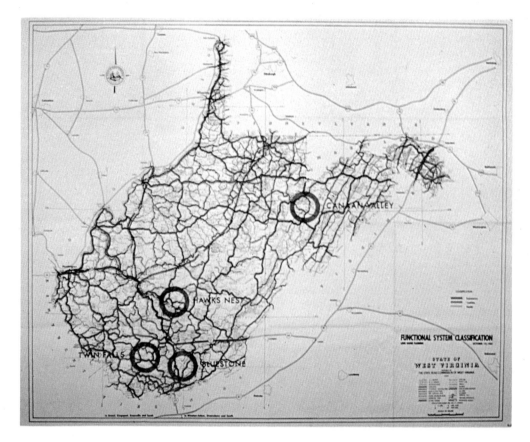

FIG. 2-32. Location of four state parks in West Virginia.

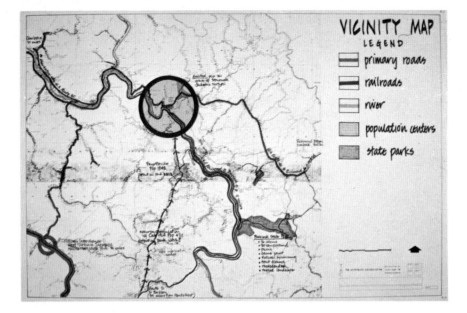

FIG. 2-33. Location of Hawk's Nest State Park.

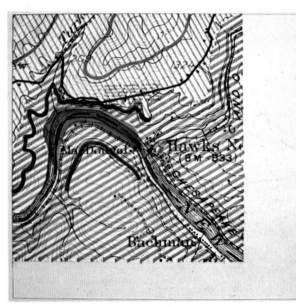

FIG. 2-34. Geology.

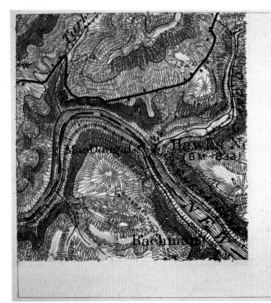

FIG. 2-35. Slope analysis.

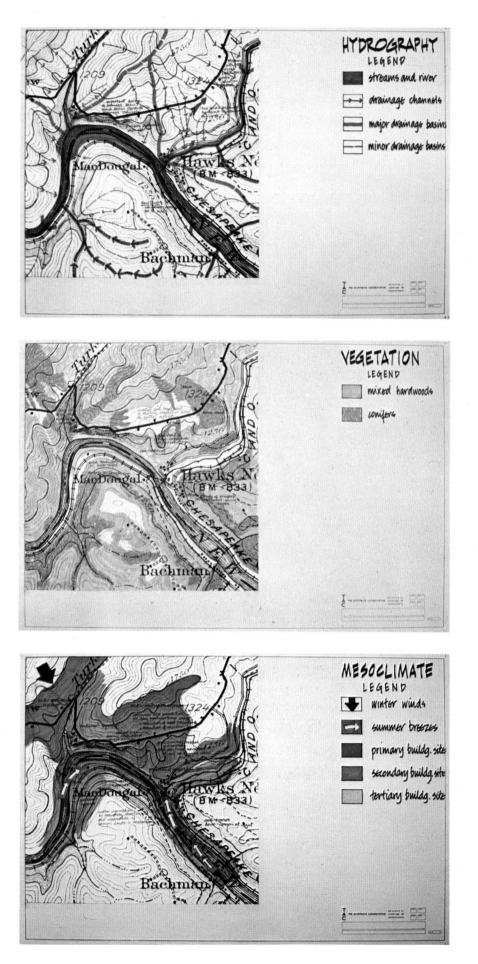

FIG. 2-36. Drainage patterns.

FIG. 2-37. Vegetation.

FIG. 2-38. Climatic factors and potential building sites.

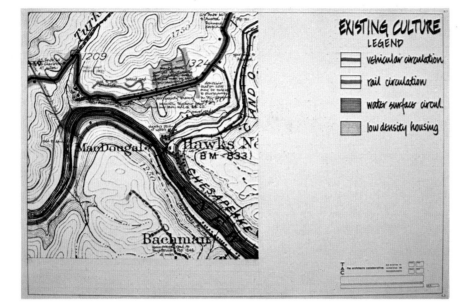

FIG. 2-39. Culture.

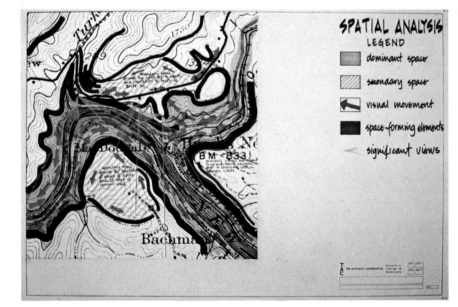

FIG. 2-40. Spatial analysis.

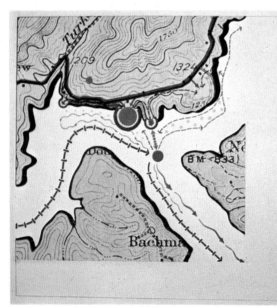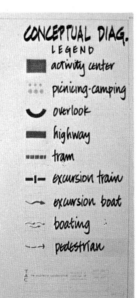

FIG. 2-41. Conceptual diagram.

West Virginia State Parks Site Analysis

This site analysis was initiated to inventory cultural, natural, and aesthetic factors to provide a factual basis for making design decisions. (See Figs. 2-32 to 2-41.)

FIG. 3-1. Pedestrian circulation as a major structuring element at Foothill College, Los Altos, Calif.

3 Land Use and Circulation

LAND USE

The land use plan evolves out of the analytical phase. (See Fig. 3-2.) It shows the general functional arrangement of a plan in terms of types of activities, linkages, and densities. Activities must be grouped so that they will function in relation to each other. When land uses have been established, the linkages between them must be evaluated. Linkages may be the movement of people, goods, or wastes, communication networks, or a connection of amenity such as views. Land use also involves the concept of density or number of families per acre. In community development plans, density standards must be adhered to.

The activities and linkages are summarized in abstract relational diagrams. Alternative diagrams must be evaluated to obtain a good solution. Value judgment, creativity, and imagination must be employed to develop these diagrams, which may be judged on linkages between activities and a sense of form and organization. If diagrams are drawn in scale with land areas, their accommodation to the actual site will become apparent. The land uses shown in abstract relational diagrams must be considered in relation to natural site features and with a general visual form in mind. They should not be forced on the site but should develop by manipulation or rearrangement of uses which keep functional relationships and linkages and also adapt to physical site conditions.

The type of construction will also influence the land use plan. If a plan is not economically feasible because of excessive site work, an alternative may be necessary. On the other hand, the type of construction may be a major factor in determining a particular land use and may require a specific type of site which is flat, rolling, or hilly. (See Figs. 3-3 to 3-5.)

CIRCULATION

Circulation systems are vital linkages which relate activities and uses on the land. The vehicular circulation system in particular produces one of the primary structuring elements of a land use plan. This system forms a hierarchy of flow or change of scale from major to minor roads within a project and also connects with off-site networks bringing people and goods to the site. On the site, and in conjunction with buildings or recreational activities, the circulation pattern must solve the difficulties of approach, drop-off and parking, and service, all in a clear and organized sequence.

One of the site planner's major concerns is the development of the vehicular and pedestrian circulation systems, but utility and communication networks are directly related to road and walk patterns. For a unified comprehensive design to be achieved, pipe lines for water and sewage, gas, oil, power, and telephone transmission must be interrelated with all elements on the site. Often utility and communication lines are placed underground; however, telephone and electric power lines are frequently elevated. Economics may influence the final decision between alternatives.

After the over-all importance of circulation is examined patterns and criteria of arrangement and development should be pursued in depth. The following examples show some of the analysis studies that were made for the expansion of an existing university. Among them were existing vehicular and pedestrian circulation plans which influenced the land use plan. Alternative circulation plans were then reviewed in order to structure the land use plan. (See Figs. 3-6 to 3-10.)

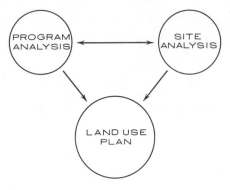

FIG. 3-2. Evolution of land use.

FIG. 3-3. Type of construction may influence the land use plan: Habitat, Expo 67.

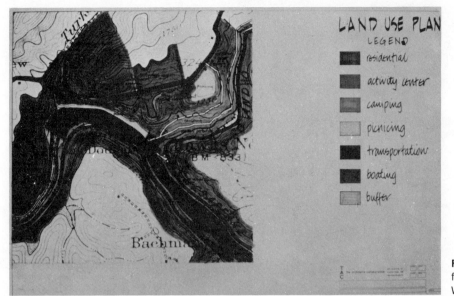

FIG. 3-4. Land use plan: this plan evolved from the analysis of Hawk's Nest State Park, West Virginia.

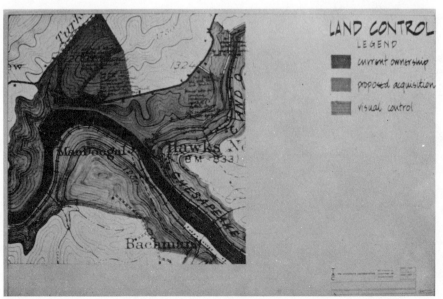

FIG. 3-5. Land control: the land use plan brought out the need for additional land acquisition to accommodate activities.

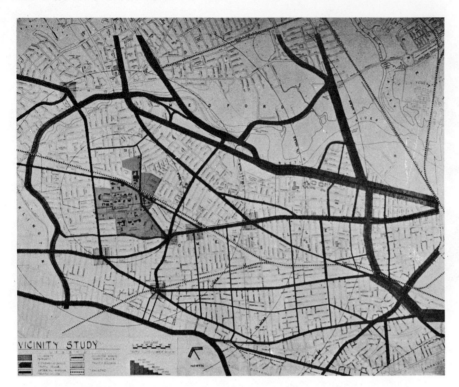

FIG. 3-6. Study map of vicinity vehicular circulation: the width of streets on this map shows the hierarchy of their use.

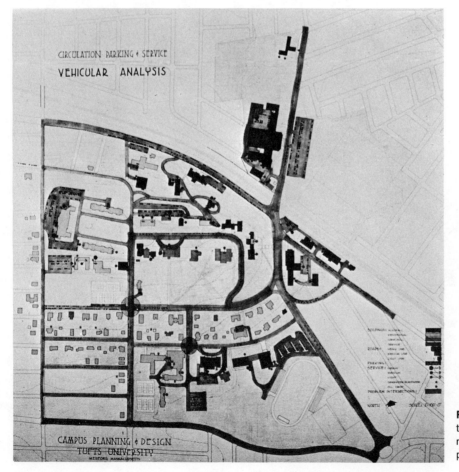

FIG. 3-7. Inventory of vehicular circulation: existing roads, parking, and service must be analyzed before future expansion proceeds.

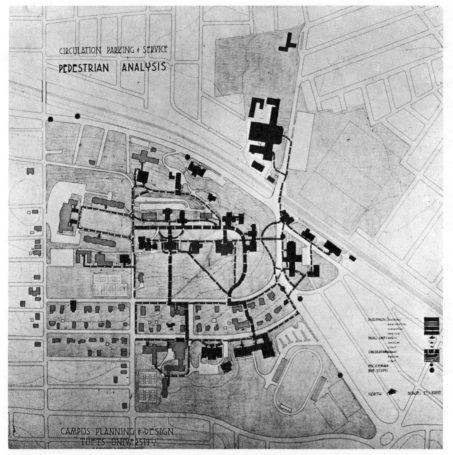

FIG. 3-8. Inventory of pedestrian circulation: an objective of this study is to determine if adequate separation exists between pedestrian and vehicular circulation.

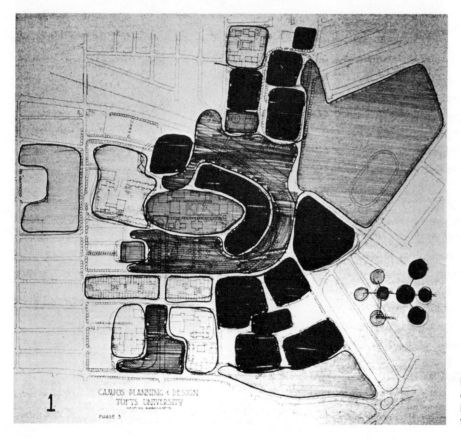

FIG. 3-9. Future land use plan: this plan developed out of the analysis phase. Designated areas are related to existing facilities and natural site features.

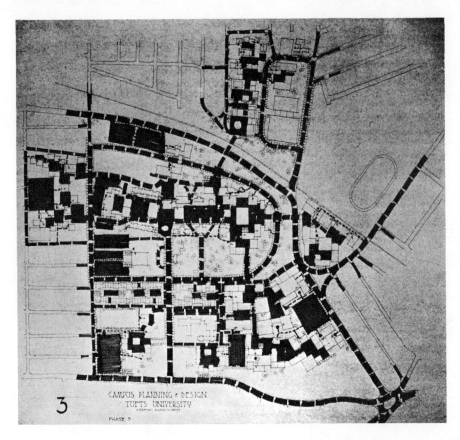

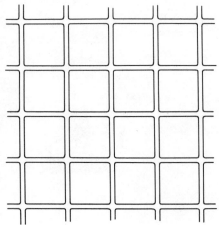

FIG. 3-10. Future-vehicular and pedestrian circulation study: this plan develops linkages necessary in carrying out the land use plan.

Vehicular Circulation Patterns

Circulation systems are not simply haphazard; they fall into categories or classifications—grid, radial, linear, or curvilinear systems, and various combinations of these.

Grid System. The grid system is usually comprised of equally spaced streets which run perpendicular to each other. Generally used on flat or slightly rolling land, it is often poorly applied and results in visual monotony or unsympathetic handling of topography.

Since grids are easy to follow, they may be used for complex distribution of flow if a hierarchy of channels is established. This hierarchy is frequently neglected, leading to confusion and overloading of some arteries. By adapting the grid to fit topography through bending, warping, varying size of blocks, and establishing a hierarchy of flow for streets, a more interesting and workable pattern may be attained. (See Fig. 3-11.)

Radial System. A radial system directs flow to a common center; where high levels of activity exist, however, the center may become hard to manage. Since its center is fixed and therefore is not easily adaptable to change, this system is not as flexible as the grid.

Rings may be added to the system which allow for by-passing of movement, and additional flow may branch out from points other than the center. Streets branching out from points along the main artery permit collection of minor distribution of flow at the local level and its direction toward the center. (See Fig. 3-12.)

Linear System. The linear system of circulation connects flow between

FIG. 3-11. Grid system.

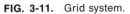

two points and is illustrated by railroad lines or canals. If movement along its length is overloaded, traffic may become impeded. An adaptation for this system is the use of loops on either side of the main artery to aid local flow. (See Fig. 3-13.)

Curvilinear System. The curvilinear system takes advantage of topography by following the land as closely as possible. This system is closely related to traffic at the local level and may have a variety of street alignments readily adaptable to topography. In a curvilinear system, there are fewer through streets as compared with the grid. Cul-de-sacs, dead-end streets having a maximum length of 500 ft., are commonly employed. All these elements have a tendency to slow traffic down. With a curvilinear system, streets are more interesting because of varied views, street types and lengths, and adaptability to topographic change. Increasingly, planned unit residential developments are adapting the curvilinear system. (See Fig. 3-14.)

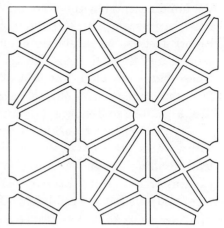

FIG. 3-12. Radial system.

Organization of Vehicular Circulation

In organizing vehicular circulation on the site, consider alternative designs in order to arrive at both a viable and aesthetically harmonious solution. Note the type of people who will be using the site. Are they employees, students, or visitors, or are they providing a service? How many will there be and, most important, will they be arriving by car, bus, or truck?

On the approaches to the site there should be a good unobstructed view of the entry drive from either direction on the highway. Sight distance varies with speed and number of lanes of highway; for example, a minimum of 200 ft. is desirable at 30 miles per hour, 275 ft. at 40 miles per hour, and 350 ft. at 50 miles per hour. Strive for a natural feeling of entry and take advantage of existing site features. Explore the site to determine whether an entry drive can be situated between large existing trees, two knolls, or other topographic forms that lend themselves to such an entry.

The alignment of roads must follow existing topography as closely as possible. Road alignment should also make use of pleasing views and existing site features on the approach drive, rather than ignoring them as often happens. Do not allow the observer's eye to slip by a building. Provide a good direct view of the building and its entry. (See Figs. 3-15 and 3-16.)

The arrival and turnaround area should be designed for a right handed drop-off. (See Figs. 3-17 and 3-18.) This permits passengers to arrive at

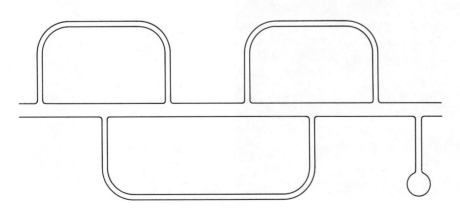

FIG. 3-13. Linear system.

the building entry without having to cross any roads. The drop-off area must be in scale with the building and designed for vehicles using it. Eighty feet is the minimum diameter desirable for automobile turn-around and drop-off areas, whereas 100 ft. or more may be desirable where buses are used. The drop-off area can be covered for protection from rain or snow, as is often done on public buildings, especially schools. (See Figs. 3-19 to 3-22.)

When insufficient transition areas occur between roads and buildings, walls, walks, steps or trees other than at drop-off areas, visual and physical crowding results. A minimum distance between paved areas and existing trees is 6 ft.; this may vary, however, depending on the size of trees and existing site conditions. If not given adequate space, trees may die because of altered site conditions to which they have not adapted. (See Figs. 3-23 and 3-24.)

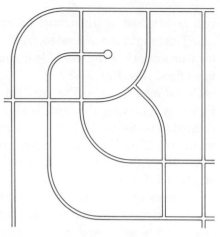

FIG. 3-14. Curvilinear system.

FIG. 3-15. The entry drive to John Deere, Moline, Ill., uses a pleasing road alignment and allows glimpses of the building on the approach.

FIG. 3-16. The natural landscape flows uninterrupted by elevating the road over existing landforms on the site at John Deere, Moline, Ill.

Visitor and Other Parking. To meet program requirements, visitor parking should link with building approach and drop-off areas and be within short walking distance of the building it serves. It should not be combined with turnaround islands or other areas that obstruct the view of a building. Visitors should not be required to arrive at a building by first driving through a parking lot. Public parking areas must have a clear connection to the entry, but those people who simply wish to park their cars directly without dropping anyone off should not have to drive past the drop-off area. Walking distance from any parking area to a facility must be as short and convenient as possible.

In shopping centers, large asphalt areas can be softened by depressing paving below grade and by using trees and other plant material. In estimating parking areas, the site planner can use 300 sq ft per car as a standard. This figure includes the parking stall plus aisles. In shopping centers, about 3 to 4 sq ft of parking space is used for each square foot of gross floor space.

Service Areas. Service areas can work in conjunction with parking facilities; it is always better, however, to separate parking and service to reduce conflict of use. Since there must be adequate maneuvering space, design for the largest service vehicle using the site. Locate service areas so that they do not block any major views. It is most important not to block entry and turnaround areas by close proximity of truck service. (See Figs. 3-25 and 3-26.)

Street Widths.

Minor streets	9 –11 ft per lane
Major streets	10 –14 ft per lane
Collector streets such as boulevards	10 –18 ft per lane
Parallel parking in addition to street	8 –10 ft per side
Private drives	8 – 9 ft per lane
Service drives	12 –14 ft in width

Turning Radii

Minor streets	12½ –15 ft radius
Major arteries used by large trucks	35 –50 ft radius

Street Intersections. Street intersections are shown in Figs. 3-28 to 3-32.

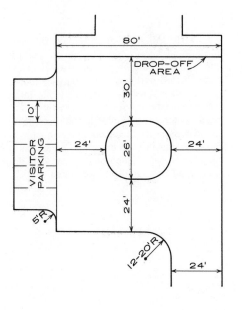

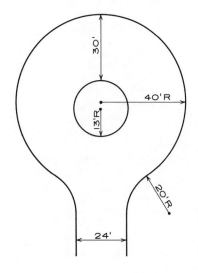

FIG. 3-17. Rectilinear drop-off area.

FIG. 3-18. Curvilinear drop-off area.

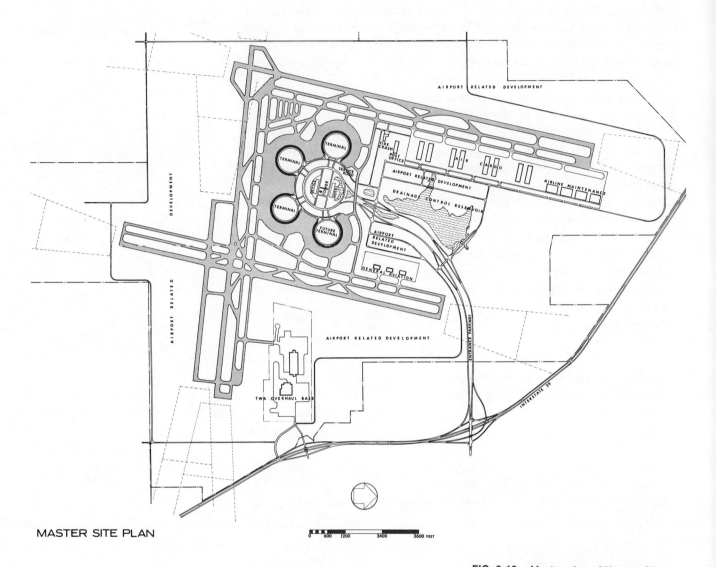

MASTER SITE PLAN

0 600 1200 2400 3600 FEET

FIG. 3-19. Master plan of Kansas City International Airport, Mo. The penetration of the landscape into the terminal areas plays a significant part in giving the passenger pleasant views on the approach to his gate. Three passenger terminals, each with 15 gates, will be constructed in the first phase of development. This concept also provides for ease of vehicular and pedestrian circulation, which includes a short walking distance from parking to terminals.

FIG. 3-20. This model of a typical terminal area clearly shows the sequence of approach, drop-off, and parking at Kansas City International Airport. The drop-off area is covered to protect passengers from rain or snow. Parking areas are depressed 4 ft below grade, which, in conjunction with a retaining wall, acts as a screening element. Five pedestrian walks radiate from the center of the parking area, giving a maximum walking distance of about 200 ft to the terminal.

FIG. 3-21. This model of Kansas City International Airport shows in further detail the design of the terminal buildings, the passenger drop-off area, the connection of the parking and terminal areas, and the use of trees to soften and add scale to the project.

FIG. 3-22. Circulation is handled very well at Dulles International Airport, Washington, D.C. There are separate levels for the enplaning and deplaning of passengers and complete separation of pedestrian and vehicular circulation from the parking level.

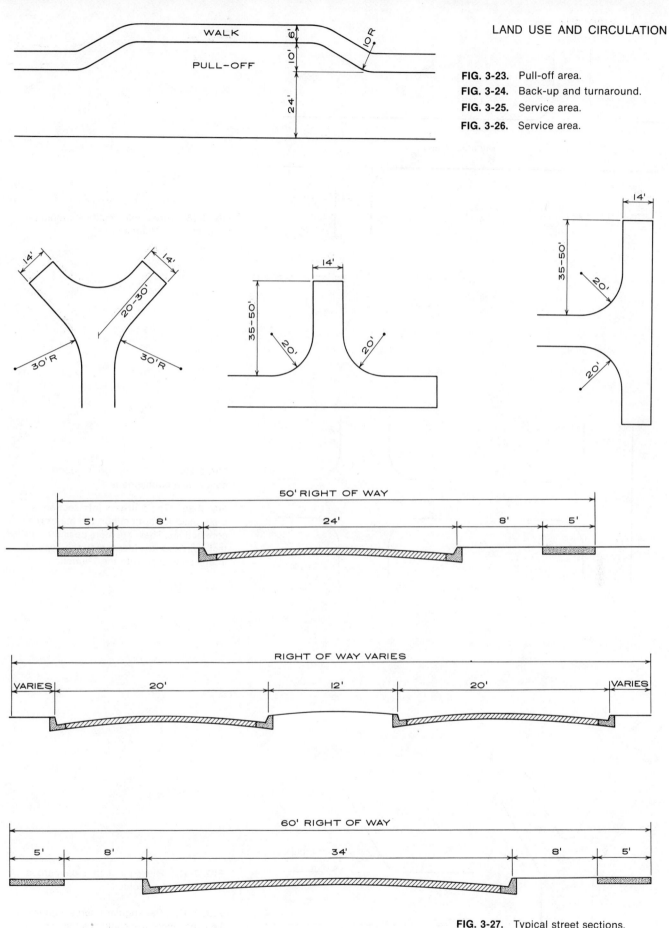

WALK

PULL-OFF

FIG. 3-23. Pull-off area.
FIG. 3-24. Back-up and turnaround.
FIG. 3-25. Service area.
FIG. 3-26. Service area.

50' RIGHT OF WAY

RIGHT OF WAY VARIES

60' RIGHT OF WAY

FIG. 3-27. Typical street sections.

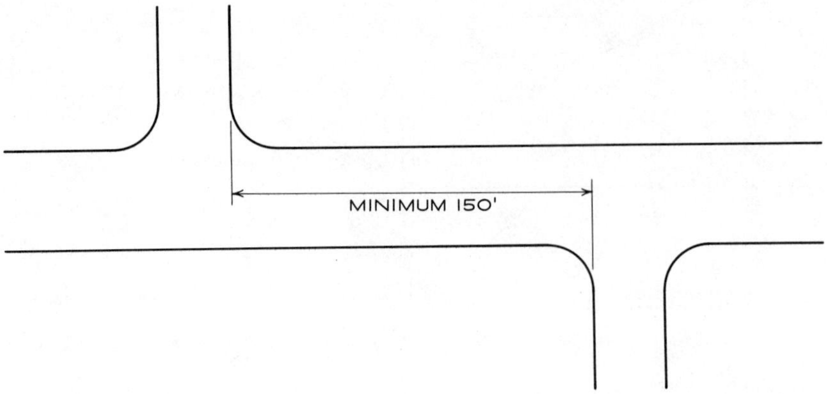

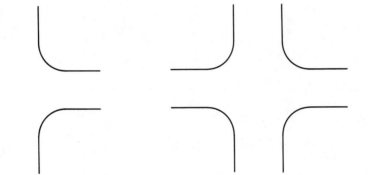

MINIMUM 150'

FIG. 3-28. Street intersections should be a minimum of 150 ft apart.

FIG. 3-29. The T-junction is good for minor road connections.

FIG. 3-30. The four-way intersection is often used for both minor and major road connections. There are more possible contact points for accidents with this type of intersection than with the T-junction.

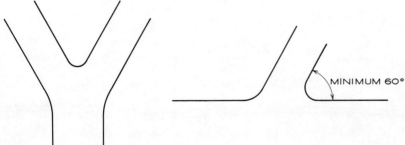

MINIMUM 60°

FIG. 3-31. The Y-junction is dangerous and should be avoided.

FIG. 3-32. The angular intersection may be used where the angle is a minimum of 60°.

Organization of Pedestrian Circulation

Pedestrian circulation forms an important linkage in relating activities on a site. It may be a principal structuring element, particularly where the pedestrian is given primary importance in projects such as college campuses, shopping malls, and recreation areas.

Pedestrians will generally follow the most direct path; if, however, a walk system is developed with points of visual interest, the pedestrian may take a longer route because of its added aesthetic enjoyment. When existing paths are circuitous, new ones may be worn through grass or planted areas. They may eventually be paved, but proper study of pedestrian flow would have prevented this problem.

In a pedestrian circulation system, the width of walks or plazas depends on their capacity, scale, and relation to other design elements. Although 5 ft is the average width for sidewalks, they may vary from 8 to 12 ft in width at vehicular drop-off areas or where volume or use make it necessary. On a pedestrian plaza or mall, large paved areas may be 40 ft or more to accommodate circulation.

Alignment of walks, the visual approach to a building, and the spatial sequence along the walk are significant factors in the design of pedestrian circulation. Fitting walks to topography and using natural site features to best advantage make for an aesthetically pleasing solution. Walks with long curves and short tangents are most desirable. There must also be a hierarchy of walk widths to distribute varying volumes of pedestrian traffic to its destination.

In establishing pedestrian circulation, studying these factors along with the texture and color of paving materials will lead to a harmonious relationship with other site elements. (See Figs. 3-33 to 3-35.)

Raised granite slabs form the major pedestrian circulation pattern at the University of Illinois, Chicago Campus. Incorporated with the plazas are outdoor lecture spaces which form focal points. (See Figs. 3-36 to 3-43.) 3-43.)

Steps and Ramps

Where grades become excessive, ramps or stairs must be used. The maximum number of risers per set is ten or twelve (risers are the vertical surface of the step, treads the horizontal). It is best to have a set of stairs no higher than eye level so that the pedestrian may judge the distance to the top of a landing safely. To prevent tripping over one or two stairs not easily seen, provide at least three risers. Handrails are used for five or more risers, especially where wet or icy conditions prevail.

A general rule to follow in establishing the size of risers and treads is 2 risers + tread = 26 in. This rule has evolved from the length of the average person's stride. Step dimensions commonly used are 5½ in. riser with 15 in. tread and 6 in. riser with 13½ to 14½ in. tread. Risers are seldom over 6 in. outdoors because a small tread would appear out of scale. Cheek walls are used for maintenance purposes and often lighting is incorporated with them. Illuminate tops of stair landings for safety.

Ramps. Ramps usually have an absolute minimum length of 5 ft; 6½ ft, however, has become a desirable minimum length based on a person's stride. Ramp grades under 6% are easier for people to use. The stated desirable maximum is 10%, although ramps up to 15% are sometimes used. (See Figs. 3-44 to 3-47.)

FIG. 3-33. Curvilinear walkway systems may direct pedestrian flow through campus areas and provide interest from varying alignment and sight lines: Foothill College, Los Altos, Calif.

FIG. 3-34. Curvilinear walk system: University of Colorado, Boulder.

FIG. 3-35. Angular walk systems also have interest from varying widths and sight lines: Northwest Plaza, St. Louis.

FIG. 3-36. University of Illinois, Chicago Campus.

FIG. 3-37. University of Illinois, Chicago Campus.

FIG. 3-38. University of Illinois, Chicago Campus.

FIG. 3-39. University of Illinois, Chicago Campus.

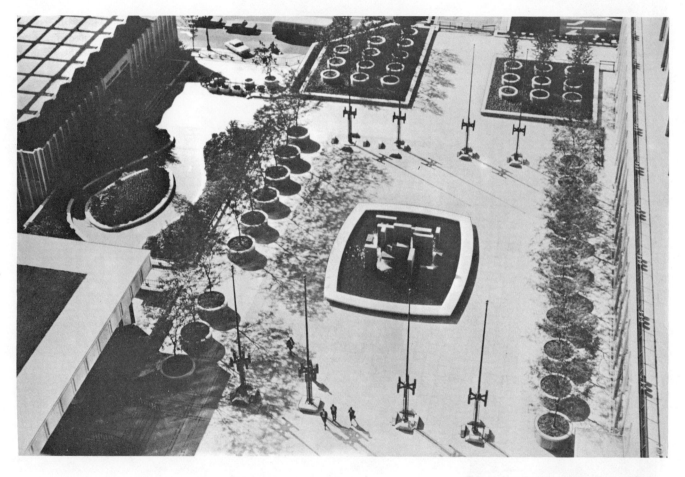

FIG. 3-40. People using the buildings defining Constitution Plaza in Hartford, Conn., have a view of the plaza, with the fountain as a focal point, from upper stories and use it as pedestrians at the plaza level.

FIG. 3-41. Covered pedestrian walkways offer protection from precipitation and the direct heat of sunlight at Stanford University, Palo Alto, Calif.

FIG. 3-42. This footbridge separates pedestrian and vehicular circulation in San Francisco.

FIG. 3-43. A footbridge crosses the canal in Busch Gardens, Sepulveda, Calif.

FIG. 3-44. The designer of these steps at the University of California, Berkeley, considered the change in grade adjacent to them.

FIG. 3-45. An outdoor stairway at the University of California, Los Angeles, acts as a focal point in the landscape.

FIG. 3-46. These steps in combination with architecture have a strong directional movement and establish an entrance sequence which leads to the quadrangle above at Wellesley College, Wellesley, Mass.

FIG. 3-47. Lighting and handrailings promote safety and are incorporated with these steps at the University of California, Santa Cruz.

Parking

Parking is one of the most important land uses on a site. It can be visually disruptive if it is not properly placed in relation to the topography and to other activities or uses. To organize parking, the site planner must be aware of the dimensions of the vehicles for which he is designing to provide adequate spaces. Include the over-all length, width, front and rear overhang, and minimum turning radii for both inside and outside front and rear bumpers.

The site planner must devise a scheme for the largest vehicle using the site (whether it be car, bus, or truck). The following factors that affect parking should be investigated. (See page 126.)

1. Size of parking area in square feet and the dimensions.
2. Angle of parking—90, 60, or 45°.
3. Direction of traffic flow to the site.
4. Type of parking—self or attendant.
5. Width of parking spaces—8½, 9, 9½, or 10 ft.
6. Width of access drive.
7. Organization of circulation within parking area, both vehicular and pedestrian—position of possible points of entrance and exit to minimize crossing movements and turns.
8. Aesthetic factors—depressing parked cars below eye level, planting, lighting, paving material.
9. Drainage of parking area.
10. Maximum walking distance from parking to building.
11. Separation of customer parking and service areas.
12. In shopping centers, parking index—amount of parking for each 1000 sq ft of gross leasable area which includes all basements, mezzanine, and floor area, 3000 to 4000 sq ft.

In some cases width of usable land determines the type of parking. A greater number of cars can be parked at 90° using same stall width than at 60 or 45°. On the other hand, 60, 45, and 30° parking establish a one-way traffic system and make it easy to pull into a space. It is more convenient and less hazardous, however, to back out of a space at 90° because of the larger aisle width.

Acute angle parking provides fewer spaces because of the curb length of the stall and the length of the space. Furthermore, there are triangular areas left over at the end of each stall and at the end of each row. If access roads and size of stalls are a minimum width, it takes a longer time to park. One-way access roads should be at least 11 ft wide, whereas two-way access should be 24 ft wide. Roads leading to parking should not be lined with cars. When people must back on to the road when leaving their parking spaces, traffic is impeded.

To open car doors easily, parking spaces 9 to 10 ft wide should be used in self-parking areas. Spaces 8 to 8½ ft in width make it necessary to squeeze in and out and are simply not convenient. (See Figs. 3-48 to 3-57.)

Both motorcycle and bicycle parking must be considered when designing circulation systems for schools, parks, and other public facilities. (See Figs. 3-58 to 3-60.)

Commonly Used Parking Dimensions[1]

Angle	Width	Curb Length	Length of Space	Aisle Width	Total
90°	9' stall	9'	19'	24'	62'
60°	9' stall	10.4'	21'	18'	60'
45°	9' stall	12.7'	19.8'	13'	52.6'

[1] Reproduced from Geoffery Baker and Bruno Funaro, *Parking*, by permission of Reinhold Book Corporation, a subsidiary of Chapman-Reinhold, Inc., New York, 1958.

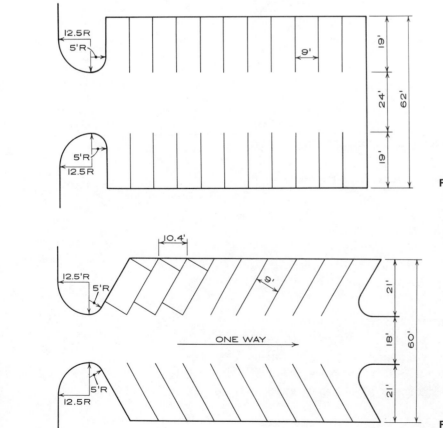

FIG. 3-48. Ninety degree parking.

FIG. 3-49. Sixty degree parking.

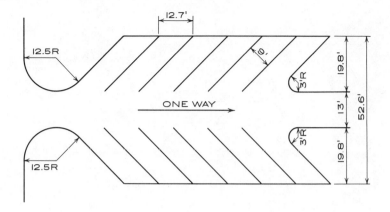

FIG. 3-50. Forty-five degree parking.

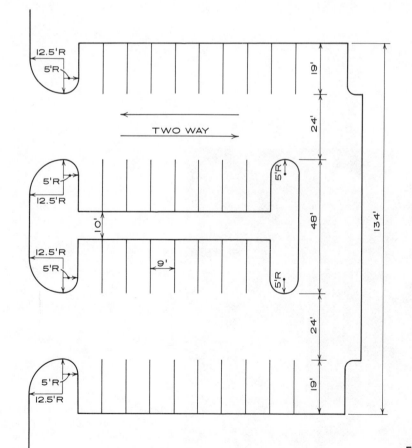

FIG. 3-51. Multi-laned 90° parking.

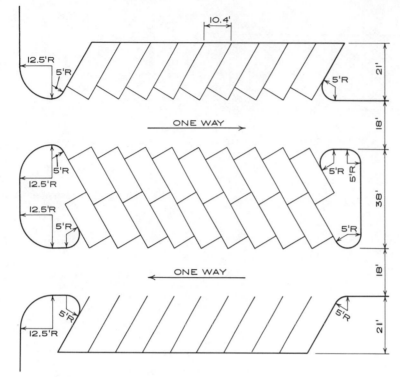

FIG. 3-52. Multi-laned 60° parking.

FIG. 3-53. Parking depressed below Lake Shore Drive, Chicago, gives an uninterrupted view of the skyline from the road.

FIG. 3-54. The front overhang on automobiles must be considered in designing pedestrian circulation. The parking is also depressed below grade and softened with planting: Kansas University, Lawrence.

FIG. 3-55. Planting and lighting are incorporated in this parking area at the University of Colorado, Boulder.

FIG. 3-56. Parking beneath these tennis courts takes advantage of limited space at the University of California, Berkeley.

FIG. 3-57. A parking garage in Denver, Colo. uses a spiral ramp system to connect the levels.

FIG. 3-58. Motorcycle parking: University of California, Los Angeles.

FIG. 3-59. Bicycle parking: University of Colorado, Boulder.

FIG. 3-60. Bicycle parking: Northwest Plaza, St. Louis.

FIG. 4-1. Studies of visual form must be made in conjunction with the land use plan.

4 Visual Design Factors and Natural Elements

VISUAL DESIGN FACTORS

Along with land use and circulation, visual design factors and natural elements must be studied in structuring the site plan. It should be viewed as a total organization of space formed with buildings, earth, rock, water, and plant material. It must be structured so that its parts not only work together but are visually unified and coherent as well.

Elements of Order

Sequence. Spaces are experienced by persons moving through them. The observer, in analyzing existing spaces, may find a planned sequence to be a very strong organizational device. Sequence is continuity in perception of spaces or objects arranged to provide a succession of visual change. It may create motion, a specific mood, or give direction. Each element in a sequence should lead to the next without necessarily revealing it.

Repetition and Rhythm. The simplest kind of sequence is repetition, which may involve color, texture, and shape; however, only a single factor must be reiterated for it to occur. (See Fig. 4-2.)

If a sequence of repetitive elements is interrupted at recurring intervals, rhythm is established. Rhythm gives variety in contrast to total repetition, which may prove monotonous. An example in an existing paving pattern would be the recurrence of brick bands between concrete squares. (See Fig. 4-3.)

Balance. The next element of order is balance. Are the objects in a space in symmetrical or asymmetrical balance? In symmetry equal and like elements are balanced on either side of an axis. Asymmetry is the balance of unequal and unlike elements on opposite sides of an axis. In occult balance an optical axis or center of gravity is implied and opposing ele-

FIG. 4-2. Repetition of design elements: Constitution Plaza, Hartford, Conn.

ments may be symmetrical or asymmetrical. An example of asymmetrical occult balance would be trees appearing to balance a hill on an implied visual axis. When opposing elements or structures develop tension among themselves, so that there seems to be a total balance of the elements along with the surrounding space, a dynamic form of balance has occurred.

Characteristics of Objects in the Landscape

Shape, Size, Scale. The characteristics of objects in the landscape determine the quality of a space and its enclosure. What is the shape or form of the space? Is it rectilinear, curvilinear, or triangular? What is the size of the space? The size of an object or space is relative; it is large or small according to the standard with which it is compared. Size also depends on the distance of an object from the observer, whereas scale denotes relative size. Scale is therefore generally based on the size of the average observer — 5 ft 9 in.

Proportion. Proportion is also a most important design factor. It is the ratio of height to width to length and may be studied in drawings or models. Shape, size, scale, and proportion in the formation of structures or spaces must be considered in design. In planning future expansion of an existing project these elements must also be studied to prevent disruption of existing areas.

FIG. 4-3. Rhythm in an existing paving pattern.

Texture and Color. Whenever one cannot determine the size and shape of specific parts as they form a continuous surface, there is texture, which may be perceived by touch or by sight. All materials used on a project have texture whether they are rough surfaced granite or smooth polished marble. Inherent in the use of materials is color. Materials must be carefully chosen to relate textures and colors. On expansion of existing projects try to match existing materials in color and texture to achieve harmony. (See Fig. 4-4.)

Hierarchy. Hierarchy may be used to rank sizes or colors. For example, a hierarchy in the sizes of spaces is a sequence of spaces which progressively change in size of importance until one comes to a dominant or central space. Another example of hierarchy is its use in determining the width of walks according to the volumes of pedestrian traffic anticipated. The third example is in ranking colors of paving material to give added importance to a dominant feature within a space, such as a fountain or sculpture. Often a darker colored material is used as a subtle transition to emphasize the paving around the feature. (See Fig. 4-5.)

Volumes and Enclosure

To achieve clearly defined spaces, consider enclosure or space-forming elements and the volumes contained by the space. Exterior volumes are formed by three enclosing or space-forming elements—the base plane, the overhead plane, and the vertical plane.

Base Plane. The base plane is our greatest concern in determining land use. It is the surface of the earth and therefore must be properly planned for uses and their linkages before further development can take place. Through treatment of the base plane, one relates and articulates all elements on its surface. A strong land use plan must exist beforehand.

Overhead Plane. The sky is our greatest overhead plane. Man-made planes may be used for further definition in the height of a space. Overhead planes may be solid, translucent, or perforated, but this is generally not as important visually as the type of articulation they provide.

Vertical Plane. Vertical planes have the most important function in articulating the uses of spaces. Buildings are usually the dominant vertical elements that articulate space and with which the site planner must work. The placement of these buildings and other vertical elements will determine the degree of enclosure of a space.

Vertical elements also have great visual impact and may act as points of reference or landmarks. A vertical element such as a sculpture may

FIG. 4-4. Harmony is achieved by repetition of design elements in this expansion of the University of Colorado at Boulder.

FIG. 4-5. Hierarchy in sizes and importance of spaces.

also become the dominant feature within a volume. Vertical planes can act as screens to eliminate objectionable views, thereby enframing good views. These planes also serve as buffering elements for noise in the form of plant material and they may control sunlight or wind. (See Figs. 4-6 to 4-8.)

NATURAL ELEMENTS

Early in the development of a site plan the planner must relate a materials concept to his spatial concept. As the spatial concept is refined, so is the materials concept. Materials have inherent characteristics that must be expressed. They are also used in conjunction with other materials and must be carefully chosen in relation to each other.

Natural elements studied in the materials concept may be earth, rock, water, or plant material. These elements are perpetually undergoing change. Variety resulting from their size, shape, texture, or color can produce an appreciable emotional effect when properly used.

Earth

Earth, the base plane upon which we build, is a plastic element and can be molded to enhance a design, especially where the topography is level or shapeless. Steep slopes left as undeveloped woodland tend to organize space and form linkages with areas adjacent to the site. In a new development existing topography often must be changed, but transition between new and existing landforms is essential. Design grading may change these existing forms to screen objectionable views, to gain privacy, or, by sinking or depressing roads, walks, and parking, to make land appear to flow undisturbed. Level and uninteresting topography can be given variety by mounding.

Studying topography in model form, whether in cardboard, clay, or some other material, is extremely valuable, for landform is difficult to interpret in a two-dimensional plan. Creating site models is a worthwhile aid to studying buildings in their relation to the land, to each other, and to influences on adjacent sites.

Rock

Rock is a prominent element in design because of its symbolic, structural, and aesthetic qualities. It may be used as a natural feature or a sculptural element. Rock composed in courtyards or gardens should have the same soil line as it had in its natural state and, if moss is present, the same orientation, moisture, and shade.

Rock that is indigenous to a site can be used to great advantage in its natural state as outcrops, ledges, or boulders as well as in walls, sculptures, podia, or buildings themselves. Taking the naturalistic approach, if the stone is used for both a structure and other site elements the building may become unified with the site through proper handling. On the other hand, the man-made approach can be emphasized by placing the building on a podium and having the natural landscape lead to the man-made structure. Either approach may work; it is up to the planner to decide which method is appropriate on the given site.

Man-made materials such as brick or concrete created from natural ele-

FIG. 4-6. Overhead planes articulate the height of a space: Busch Gardens, Sepulveda, Calif.

73

ments can also be classified as rock. These are widely used in construction and detailing.

Water

Water, the most flexible of natural elements, assumes the shape of its container. It is like a magnet in the landscape, drawing people toward it. Giving a cooling and reflective effect in large still pools, it conveys a sense of quietude and repose. Essential to the balance of life, in hot arid climates water makes living bearable. Differences in sound also make its use appealing. Water in fountains or pools may splash, drip, gurgle, trickle, foam, flood, pour, spurt, ripple, surge, spray, or jet. Fountains of various sizes may be designed to take advantage of a particular sound. Sunlight and night lighting add other qualities and are important considerations in fountain design. Finally, water may produce a feeling of coherence in a design when used or found naturally in large bodies, for it acts as a unifying element.

Plant Material

Plants constantly undergo change, especially during peaks of seasonal variation; this makes the use of plant material most challenging. Trees or shrubs can stand out as sculptural elements in the landscape or be used en masse for enclosure, to screen objectionable views, give privacy or protection from noise or winter wind, form a backdrop, or give shelter overhead by providing shade in summer. Groundcovers, including grass, are not only used as surfacing elements but control erosion and provide variety with color and texture.

Criteria Affecting Selection of Plant Material

Hardiness

1. Is a specific tree, shrub, or groundcover hardy in the region of the country where the site is located? Hardiness depends primarily on temperature and precipitation; however, soil properties such as degree of acidity or alkalinity are also important factors to consider.
2. Does the tree, shrub, or groundcover grow in or withstand moist or dry soil?
3. Will it tolerate city conditions if required? When the tree is too close to paved areas, will it die? When the tree is adjacent to paved areas, will it damage the paving?
4. Does it provide shade or does it have light and airy foliage?
   shade? Does it prefer south or north slopes? South slopes sometimes thaw in winter and this may cause damage to roots of some trees.
5. Is the tree, shrub, or groundcover free of or easily susceptible to disease?

Form and Structure

1. What is the height and spread of tree or shrub at maturity? How long does it take to reach maturity?
2. Is the tree, shrub, or groundcover deciduous or evergreen? Deciduous trees may provide shade in summer and allow sunlight through in winter. Evergreen trees provide color year round and are good for windbreaks or screens.
3. Does the tree have good branch structure and bark color?
4. Does it provide shade or does it have light and airy foliage?

Foliage, Flowers, and Fruit

1. What is the foliage size, form, texture, and color?
2. Is there autumn color? To what degree?
3. Are the flowers or fruits significant? When do they occur? How long do they remain effective on the plant? What is their color? Are the flowers fragrant?

Care

1. Is the tree, shrub, or groundcover easy or difficult to transplant?
2. Does it require much or little maintenance?

Arrangement

Provided plant selection criteria are met, plant material native to the site's region may be used or it may be imported from other areas. Both plant selection and arrangement must follow a planting plan developed to solve functional and aesthetic problems. Arrangement is based upon the relation of plants in size, form, texture, and color. The site planner knows which plants to group together by studying natural plant relationships (ecology) and trying to group them similarly in his scheme, or after becoming familiar with the palette of plants and comprehending their size, form, texture, and color, he may form his own arrangement based on one or several of their characteristics. He could, for example, group flowering trees by color and time of bloom.

Plant material may also be grouped in relation to topography, or to architectural structure or it may form a transition between ground and structure. It can become an enclosure or shelter, provide a screen, block wind, or offer shade. Particular trees serve to fulfill these needs much better than others, and it is the designer's knowledge and experience in using plant materials which serves best in the final analysis.

FIG. 4-8. Vertical elements such as planters and trees, along with a change in paving material, articulate this space on Constitution Plaza, Hartford, Conn.

FIG. 5-1. Architecture in a refined setting accomplished by changing existing contours in the design grading phase: Connecticut General Insurance Company.

5 Contour Lines

A planner must understand the characteristics of contours to develop the site plan. Contours facilitate his visualization of land in the third dimension. They show existing elevations of topography and comprise a contour map which will reveal site characteristics.

The primary purpose for changing existing contours is to direct runoff water away from structures or activity areas and to adapt man-made structures to existing topography. This process is called grading and is discussed in Chapter 6. The following definitions introduce the nature of contour lines; plotting contours is also described in this chapter.

Contour Characteristics

Contours are lines of equal elevation above the same reference plane. The *datum plane* is the reference generally referred to and is located at mean sea level. A *contour interval* is the vertical distance between contours, and the choice of a suitable interval results from the purpose for which a topographic map is to be used. Common intervals are 1, 2, and 5 ft.

Knowledge of the characteristics of contours is essential for their interpretation. A list of them follows.

1. A uniform slope is indicated by evenly spaced contours. (See Fig. 5-2.)

2. Slope increases with closeness of contours. When the lines are close at the top of a slope and wider apart at the bottom, they indicate a concave slope. The reverse situation indicates a convex slope. (See Fig. 5-3.)

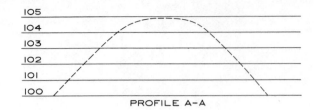

PROFILE A-A

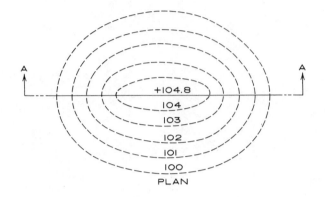

+104.8

104

103

102

101

100

PLAN

FIG. 5-2. Contours show uniform slopes.

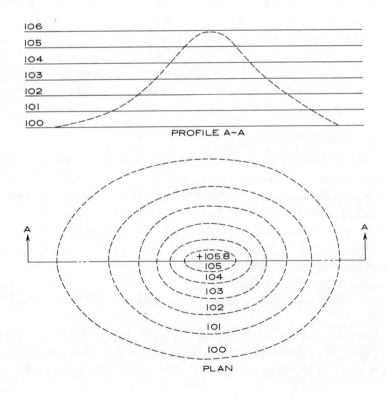

PROFILE A-A

+105.8
105
104
103
102
101
100

PLAN

FIG. 5-3. Contours show concave slopes.

3. Contour lines point up stream valleys. (See Fig. 5-4.)

4. Contour lines point down ridges. (See Fig. 5-5.)

5. With the exception of an overhanging shelf or cave, contours never cross; they merge only at vertical walls or cliffs.

6. Contours along the highest points of ridges or the lowest points of valleys are always found in pairs, for each contour is a continuous line that closes on itself, either on or off the drawing, and never splits or stops. (See Fig. 5-6.)

7. High points on summits or low points within a depression are indicated by spot elevations.

8. Runoff water flows downhill perpendicular to contour lines. (See Fig. 5-7.)

9. Existing contours are shown as dashed lines with every sixth line in a 1 ft contour interval drawn heavier. Contours are numbered either in the mass of the contour line or on the uphill side. New contour lines for proposed grades are shown as solid lines. (See Fig. 5-8.)

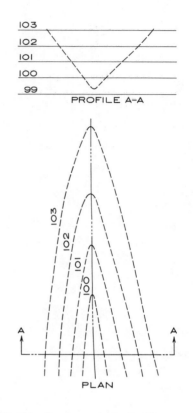

FIG. 5-4. Contours show streams.

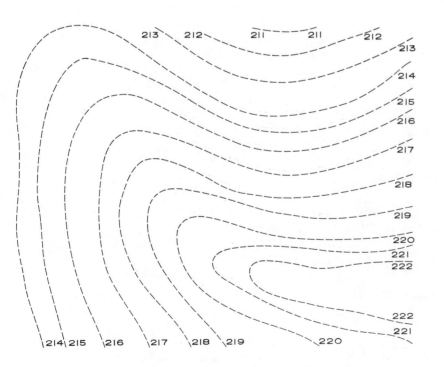

FIG. 5-5. Contours show ridges.

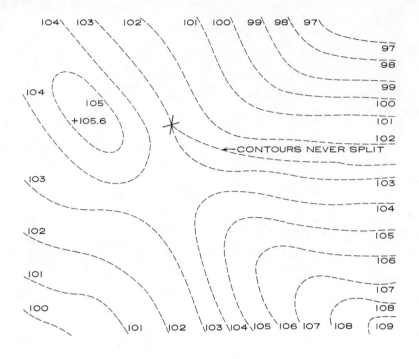

FIG. 5-6. Contours never split.

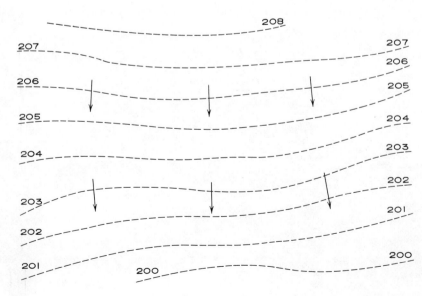

FIG. 5-7. Contour lines show flow of runoff water.

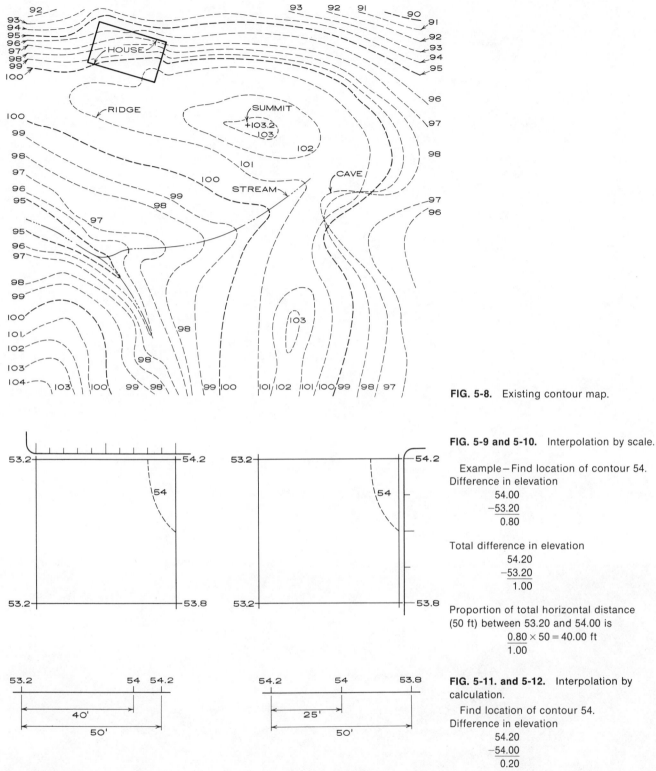

FIG. 5-8. Existing contour map.

FIG. 5-9 and 5-10. Interpolation by scale.

Example—Find location of contour 54.
Difference in elevation

$$\begin{array}{r} 54.00 \\ -53.20 \\ \hline 0.80 \end{array}$$

Total difference in elevation

$$\begin{array}{r} 54.20 \\ -53.20 \\ \hline 1.00 \end{array}$$

Proportion of total horizontal distance (50 ft) between 53.20 and 54.00 is

$$\frac{0.80 \times 50}{1.00} = 40.00 \text{ ft}$$

FIG. 5-11. and 5-12. Interpolation by calculation.

Find location of contour 54.
Difference in elevation

$$\begin{array}{r} 54.20 \\ -54.00 \\ \hline 0.20 \end{array}$$

Total difference in elevation

$$\begin{array}{r} 54.20 \\ -53.80 \\ \hline 0.40 \end{array}$$

Proportion of total horizontal distance

(50 ft) between 53.80 and 54.00 is

$$\frac{0.20 \times 50}{0.40} = 25 \text{ ft}$$

Interpolation of Contours

Interpolation of contours is the process of establishing even numbered contours from a grid system of spot elevations measured by a surveyor. In some cases he has already done this; however, the site planner may need additional elevations and these are found by interpolation either with a scale (see Figs. 5-9 and 5-10) or by calculation (see Figs. 5-11 and 5-12).

FIG. 6-1. Mounding created in Prospect Park, Brooklyn, provides a strong directional movement in the space.

6 Grading and Earthwork Calculations

GRADING

A concept of design grading is essential in developing the physical form of the site. This grading concept must strengthen the over-all project rather than detracting from it, as often happens. Positive drainage, a most important concept in grading, allows storm water runoff to flow away from structures and activity areas. When water flows away from structures toward drainage channels, flooding is prevented. Studying existing and proposed topography in model form will aid in relating buildings or activities to the land. It is also especially helpful in observing the relationship between ground forms such as mounds when this type of treatment is desired. (See Figs. 6-2 to 6-8.)

Definitions of Terms Commonly Used in Grading

Grade: Percentage of rise or fall per 100 ft. (See Fig. 6-9.)

Crown: Provides for runoff of water on roads or walks. Symbol x in Fig. 6-10 indicates crown; it may be in inches per foot or a whole number (6 in. crown).

Cross Slope or Pitch: Provides for runoff on paved areas and is given in inches per foot or a whole number.

Wash: Provides for runoff on steps and is given in inches per foot (⅛ in. to ¼ in.). (See Fig. 6-11.)

Batter: Amount of deviation from vertical such as 2 in. per ft for a vertical surface such as a wall—2:1 batter. (See Fig. 6-12.)

Slope: The ratio of horizontal to vertical. (See Fig. 6-13.)

Maximum Slopes:

Solid rock	¼ : 1	Firm earth	1½ : 1
Loose rock	½ : 1	Soft earth	2 : 1
Loose gravel	1½ : 1	Mowing grass	3 : 1

Cut and Fill: When a proposed contour is moved back into an existing slope, cut is indicated. When a proposed contour is moved away from an existing slope, fill is indicated. It is the purpose of earthwork calculation to determine if a balance exists between cut and fill or whether material

FIG. 6-2. These mounds act as islands in this garden at Constitution Plaza, Hartford. The base plane of the garden is crowned to permit runoff water to flow toward the moat surrounding the garden where it is inconspicuously picked up in drains.

FIG. 6-3. The mounds are defined by the coping at seating height. They also permit trees to be planted above the parking garage at Constitution Plaza, Hartford.

FIG. 6-4. Mounds act as islands floating on the paved areas at Southern Illinois University, Edwardsville. Their placement also provides a feeling of entry.

will have to be added to or carried away from the site. (See Fig. 6-14.)

Spot Elevations

The grading plan is the most important study in the technical development of the site plan. The major consideration in a grading plan is to set trial or preliminary spot elevations in order to achieve a positive drainage pattern. This study follows development of the land use and circulation plans, along with studies in visual form, and is done on the topographic map with requirements established in Chapter 2. Before the grading study begins the project's layout has already been drawn on the topographic map, used as the base sheet. This study may lead to changes in placement of the building or circulation.

FIG. 6-5. This sunken garden is formed by man-made berms at Expo 67.

FIG. 6-6. The base plane slopes so that runoff water may flow toward catch basins located in the paved drainage swale. This swale becomes part of the over-all paving pattern at Southern Illinois University, Edwardsville.

Factors to Consider in Setting Preliminary Spot Elevations

1. Setting the first floor elevations of buildings, generally a minimum of 6 in. above grade.
2. Meeting existing building elevations and relating grading to adjacent properties so as not to disturb by regrading or diversion of runoff.
3. Relating elevations of roads, walks, parking, and other activities to building elevations to achieve positive drainage.
4. Saving good trees by taking their elevation into consideration, or planning on the use of tree wells in cuts of 6 in. or fills over 12 in.
5. Avoiding rock or drainage problems by careful examination of the site.

FIG. 6-7. The Performing Arts Center at Saratoga Springs, N. Y., makes use of the natural slope of the land for the seating area; the raised pedestrian walkway allows the landscape to flow undisturbed.

FIG. 6-8. The grading of this slope is too steep and has caused erosion.

6. Saving the cost of unnecessary retaining walls where other types of grading concepts may be used.

7. General balancing of cut and fill areas so that material will not have to be hauled to or from the site.

After preliminary spot elevations are studied in relation to each other, preliminary contour lines are drawn on the grading plan at a chosen contour interval such as 1, 2, or 5 ft. When the proper balance of cut and fill has been obtained, final spot elevations and contour lines are set.

Finished Spot Elevations Are Placed at the Following Locations

1. First floor elevations of buildings.
2. All corners of buildings and door stoops or landings.
3. Corners of parking areas, terraces, or other paved areas.
4. Corners at the top of landings and bottom of steps.
5. Top and bottom of walls, curbs, and gutters.
6. On rock outcrops and bases of large trees (3-4 in. cal).
7. Rim and invert elevations of drainage structures—catch basins, manholes, drain inlets, and invert elevations of sanitary sewers and water lines.

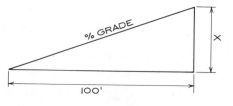

FIG. 6-9. Grade.

ROAD WIDTH
PITCH

FIG. 6-10. Crown and pitch.

Gradients

Desirable Grades	Maximum, %	Minimum, %
1. Streets	8%	0.50%
2. Parking	5	0.50
3. Service areas	5	0.50
4. Main approach walks to buildings	4	1
5. Stoops or entries to buildings	2	1
6. Collector walks	8	1
7. Ramps	10	1
8. Terraces and sitting areas	2	1
9. Grass areas for recreational use	3	2
10. Swales	10	2
11. Mowed banks of grass	3:1 slope	—
12. Unmowed banks	2:1 slope	—

1/4"/FOOT

FIG. 6-11. Wash.

Setting Grades for Positive Drainage

The formula $G = D/L$ is of major importance in manipulation of contours.

    G = Percent of grade
    D = Difference in elevation
    L = Horizontal length between two points

For example, $G = D/L$ as in Fig. 6-15:

$$G = \frac{2 \text{ ft}}{200 \text{ ft}}$$
$$G = 1\%$$

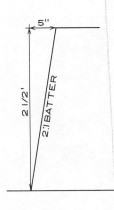

FIG. 6-12. Batter.

Establishing Contours

Set the contours at a 1 ft contour interval on Fig. 6-16.
In setting contours D = the distance between contours at a particular grade and contour interval. (See pages 100 to 103.)

$$D = \frac{CI}{\%G} \times 100$$

    CI = Contour interval
    $\%G$ = Percent of grade

$$D = \frac{1 \text{ ft}}{2.4} \times 100$$
$$D = 41.6 \text{ ft}$$

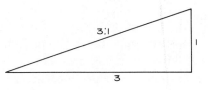

In Fig. 6-17 corner A has an elevation of 102.5 ft with a ¼ in./ ft cross slope toward corner B, and corner C has an elevation of 100.1 ft with a ¼ in./ft cross slope toward corner D. Set the contours.

FIG. 6-13. Slope.

The distance between contours is 41.6 ft as in Fig. 6-16. Now calculate corner B = (¼ in./ft for 24 ft = 6 in.) 102 ft and corner D = 99.6. Draw in contours. (See pages 100 to 103.)

Contours on Slopes. See Figs. 6-18 to 6-23.

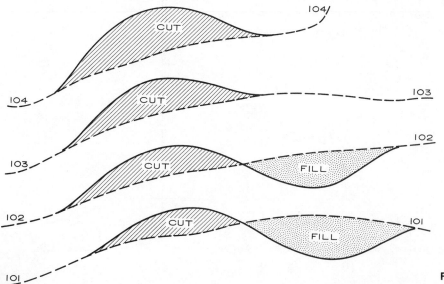

FIG. 6-14. Cut and fill.

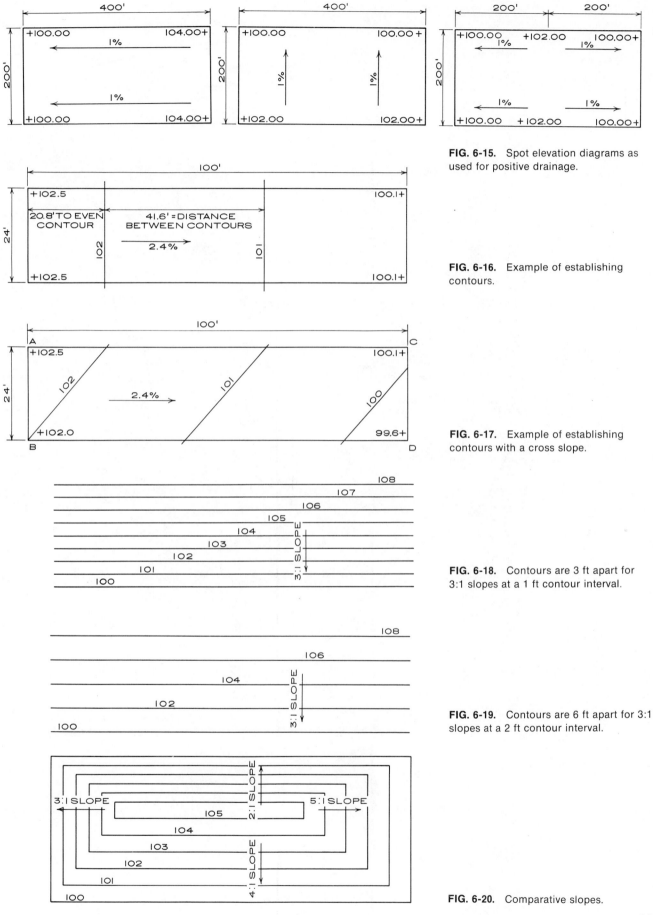

FIG. 6-15. Spot elevation diagrams as used for positive drainage.

FIG. 6-16. Example of establishing contours.

FIG. 6-17. Example of establishing contours with a cross slope.

FIG. 6-18. Contours are 3 ft apart for 3:1 slopes at a 1 ft contour interval.

FIG. 6-19. Contours are 6 ft apart for 3:1 slopes at a 2 ft contour interval.

FIG. 6-20. Comparative slopes.

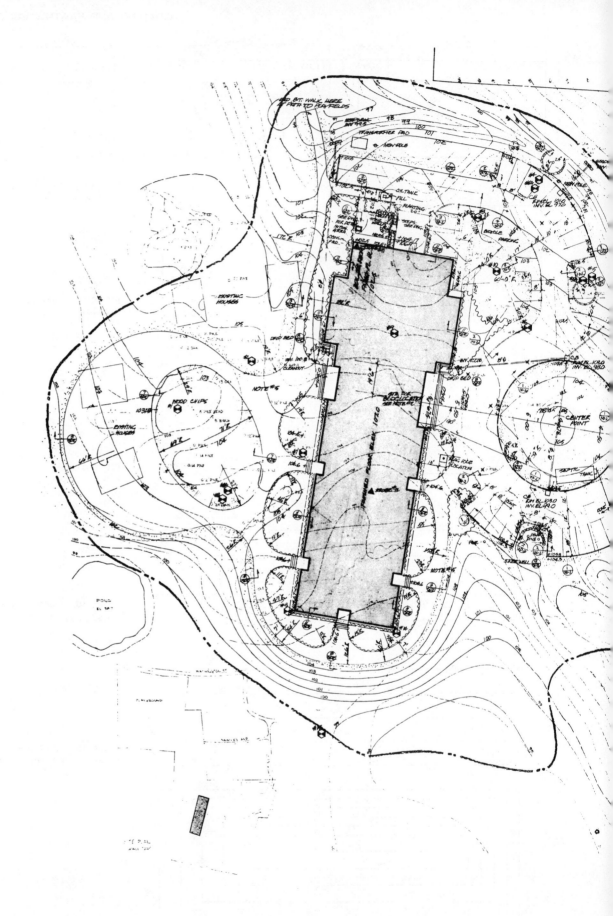

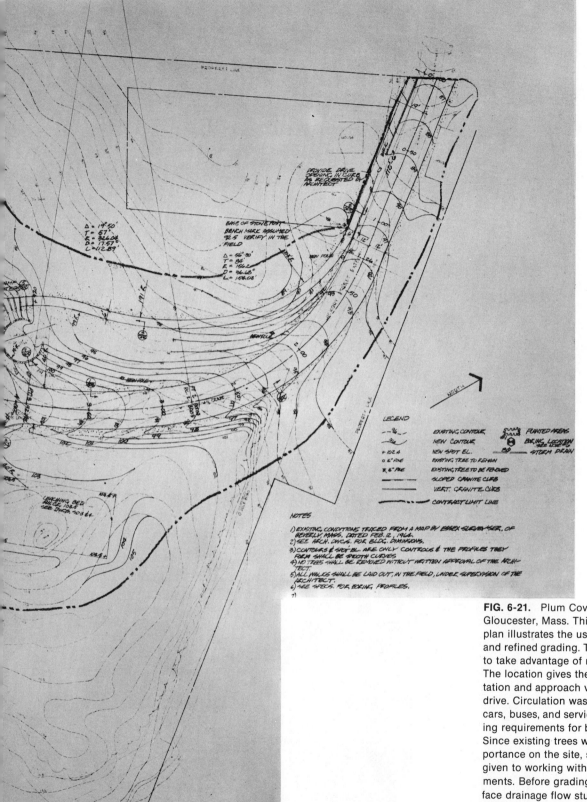

FIG. 6-21. Plum Cove Elementary School, Gloucester, Mass. This layout and grading plan illustrates the use of spot elevations and refined grading. The school was placed to take advantage of natural site features. The location gives the building good orientation and approach views from the entry drive. Circulation was developed to handle cars, buses, and service vehicles, and parking requirements for both staff and visitors. Since existing trees were of particular importance on the site, special attention was given to working with them as design elements. Before grading was started a surface drainage flow study was made to determine positive drainage. From this study trial grading plans were developed until all grades achieved the purposes of the design plan. The refined grading on the site reinforces the design and uses 3:1 slopes to blend into the existing grade on either side of the entry drive.

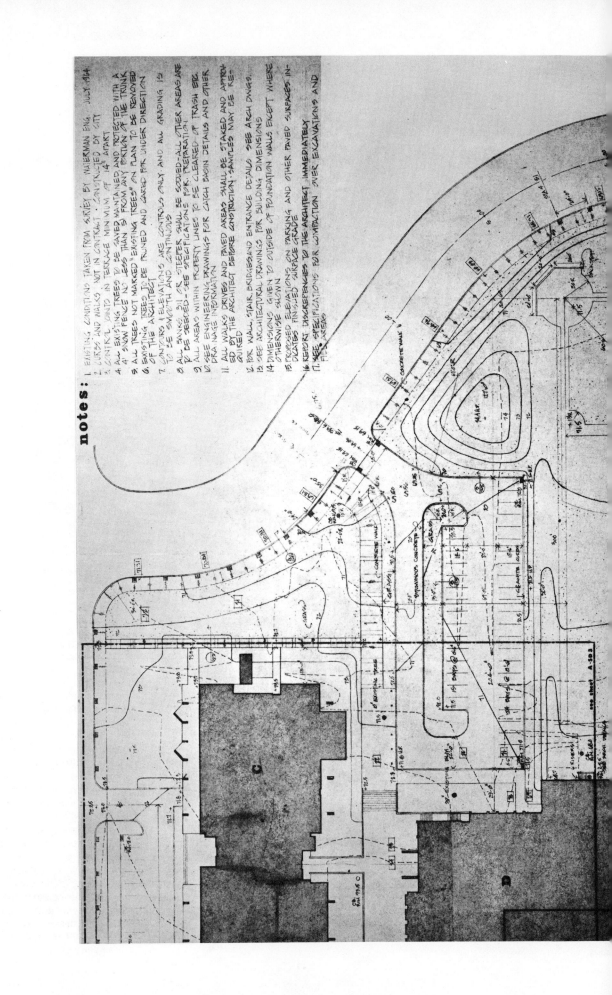

notes:

1. EXISTING CONDITIONS TAKEN FROM SURVEY BY WATERMAN ENG.   JULY 1914
2. CURBS AND WALKS NOT IN CONTRACT - CONSTRUCTED BY CITY
3. CONTRL JOINTS IN TERRACE MINIMUM OF 14" APART
4. ALL EXISTING TREES TO BE SAVED MAINTAINED AND PROTECTED WITH A 4' SNOW FENCE NO LESS THAN 5' FROM ANY PORTION OF THE TRUNK
5. ALL TREES NOT MARKED "EXISTING TREES" ON PLAN TO BE REMOVED
6. EXISTING TREES TO BE PRUNED AND GRADED FOR UNDER DIRECTION OF THE ARCHITECT
7. CONTOURS & ELEVATIONS ARE CONTROLS ONLY, AND ALL GRADING IS TO BE SMOOTH AND CONTINUOUS
8. ALL BANKS 3:1 OR STEEPER SHALL BE SODDED. ALL OTHER AREAS ARE TO BE SEEDED - SEE SPECIFICATIONS FOR PREPARATION
9. ALL AREAS WITHIN PROPERTY LINES TO BE CLEARED OF TRASH ETC.
10. SEE ENGINEERING DRAWINGS FOR CATCH BASIN DETAILS AND OTHER DRAINAGE INFORMATION
11. ALL WALKS DRIVES AND PAVED AREAS SHALL BE STAKED AND APPROVED BY THE ARCHITECT BEFORE CONSTRUCTION. SAMPLES MAY BE RE-QUIRED
12. FOR WALL, STAIR, BRIDGES AND ENTRANCE DETAILS SEE ARCH DWGS.
13. SEE ARCHITECTURAL DRAWINGS FOR BUILDING DIMENSIONS
14. DIMENSIONS GIVEN TO OUTSIDE OF FOUNDATION WALLS EXCEPT WHERE OTHERWISE SHOWN
15. FOR GOOD ELEVATIONS ON PARKING AND OTHER PAVED SURFACES IN-DICATED FINISHED SURFACE GRADE
16. REPORT DISCREPENCIES TO THE ARCHITECT IMMEDIATELY
17. SEE SPECIFICATIONS FOR COMPACTION OVER EXCAVATIONS AND FILL AREAS

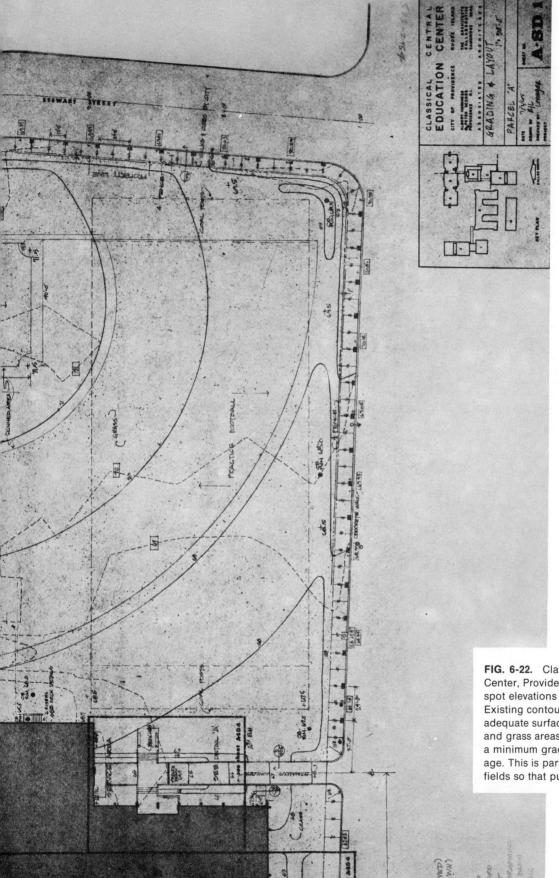

FIG. 6-22. Classical Central Education Center, Providence, R. I. Note the use of spot elevations and grading on this plan. Existing contours were changed to develop adequate surface drainage for both paved and grass areas. Grass areas should have a minimum grade of 2% for surface drainage. This is particularly important on play fields so that puddles do not occur.

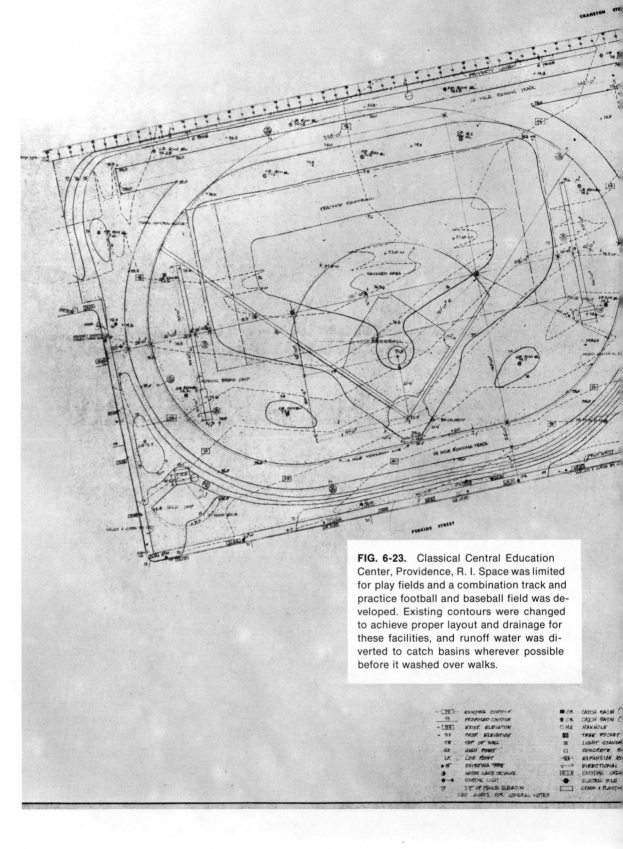

FIG. 6-23. Classical Central Education Center, Providence, R. I. Space was limited for play fields and a combination track and practice football and baseball field was developed. Existing contours were changed to achieve proper layout and drainage for these facilities, and runoff water was diverted to catch basins wherever possible before it washed over walks.

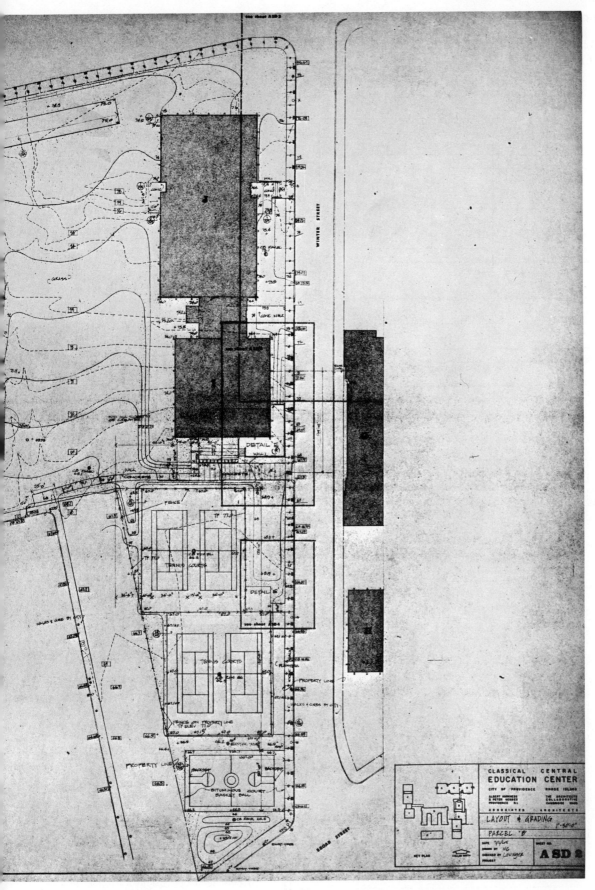

Layout and Grading of Play Fields

The dimensions of play fields (collegiate size), orientation, and spot elevations or sections of play fields are shown in Figs. 6-24 to 6-31. Sometimes dimensions of play fields will vary according to the age group or sex which uses them.

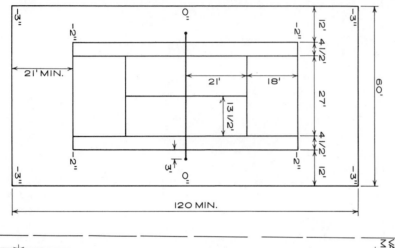

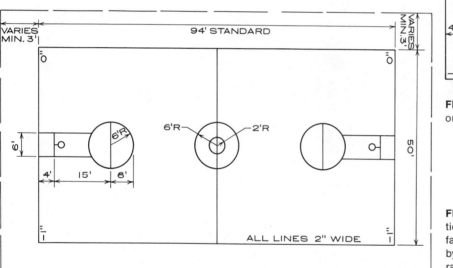

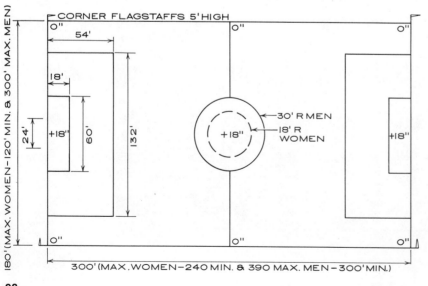

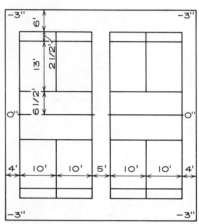

FIG. 6-24. Tennis courts: for positive drainage of tennis courts the playing surface should slope away from the net. Orientation should be handled with the courts on a north-south axis, net 3 ft high.

FIG. 6-25. Badminton: north-south orientation, with net 5 ft high.

FIG. 6-26. Basketball: north-south orientation with basket 10 ft above the ground. A fan-shaped backboard is used which is 35 by 54 in.; the top corners have a 29 in. radius. The top of the backboard is 12 ft 8 in. above the playing surface.

FIG. 6-27. Soccer: men's and women's soccer field dimensions vary; the field shown here is acceptable in over-all dimensions for both sexes.

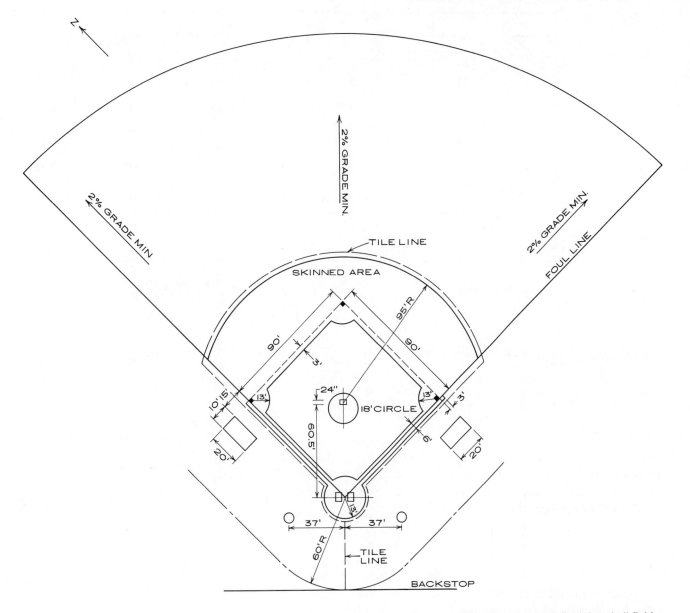

FIG. 6-28. Baseball field: baseball fields have foul lines of 300 ft or more. Softball is similar in layout to baseball with bases 60 ft apart. The distance from the back edge of the pitching rubber to home plate is 40 ft. Foul lines are 250 ft long.

FIG. 6-29. Section showing grading of infield.

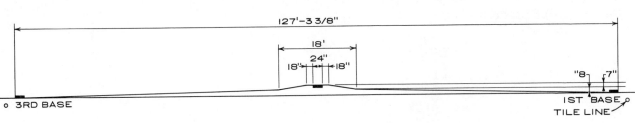

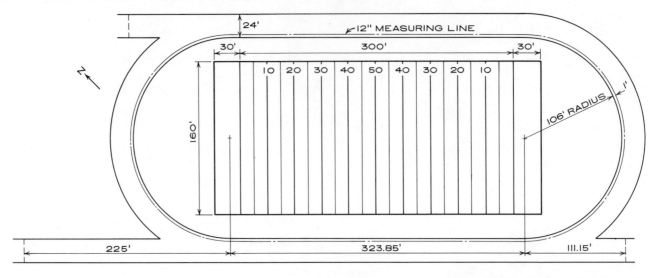

FIG. 6-30. Track and football field: the track has four laps per mile.

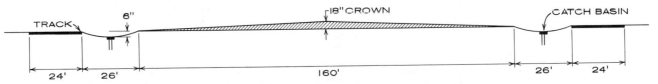

FIG. 6-31. Section showing grading of football field. The center of the field has a crown of 18 in. This is the minimum that should be used for proper drainage.

Contours on Roads

The formulas $G = D/L$ and $D = CI/\%G \times 100$ are used extensively in calculating contours on roads. Roads may have a crown or cross slope for drainage of storm water runoff. To calculate crown, shoulder, or ditch, use the following formula:

$$\frac{X}{CI} = \frac{TD}{D} \quad \text{or} \quad TD = \frac{X \times D}{CI}$$

TD = Travel distance, the measurement needed to indicate contours for crown, shoulder, or ditch.

X = A difference in elevation due to cross slope, ditch depth, etc.

D = Distance between contours at a particular grade and contour interval.

CI = Contour interval.

The following examples will illustrate the use of these formulas. A road 20 ft wide has a crown of ½ in. per ft, a 7% grade, a 5 ft shoulder with a ¼ in. per ft pitch away from the road, a ditch 6 ft wide and 6 in. deep, and a contour interval of 1 ft. Plot the crossing of three contours on the road.

1. Draw a plan of the road at a scale of your choosing.
2. The grade is given as 7%; establish the distance between contours. Since this example is not related to topography, pick any point to start from along the road center line.

$$D = \frac{CI}{\%G} \times 100$$

$$D = \frac{1}{7} \times 100$$

$$D = 14.28 \text{ ft}$$

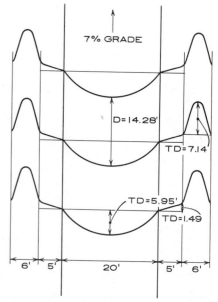

FIG. 6-32. Contours on roads.

3. Establish crown—crown = ½ in. per ft for half the road width of 20 ft.

$$Crown = 5 \text{ in.}$$

Find the travel distance for the crown.

$$TD = \frac{X}{CI} \times D$$

$$TD = \frac{5 \text{ in.}}{12 \text{ in.}} \times 14.28 \text{ ft}$$

$$TD = 5.95 \text{ ft}$$

The crown which points downhill is now set.

4. Draw shoulder width on the plan. The shoulder = ¼ in. per ft for 5 ft and slopes away from the road.

$$Shoulder = 1\tfrac{1}{4} \text{ in.}$$

Now find the travel distance for the shoulder and set it on the plan.

$$TD = \frac{X}{CI} \times D$$

$$TD = \frac{1.25 \text{ in.}}{12 \text{ in.}} \times 14.28 \text{ ft}$$

$$TD = 1.49 \text{ ft}$$

5. Draw the ditch width on the plan. The ditch depth was given as 6 in.

$$Ditch = 6 \text{ in.}$$

We must now find the travel distance for the ditch and set it on the plan. (See Fig. 32.)

$$TD = \frac{X}{CI} \times D$$

$$TD = \frac{6 \text{ in.}}{12 \text{ in.}} \times 14.28 \text{ ft}$$

$$TD = 7.14 \text{ ft}$$

A road 20 ft wide has a 6 in. crown, 6 in. curbs, and 6 ft walk (left side) with ¼ in. cross slope away from the road. The side slopes along the road are 3:1. Plot 2 ft contours on the road. The scale is 1 in. = 20 ft and station elevations are given.

1. Start at station 3 + 00 and elevation 24.35 ft given on the plan. Determine the grade.

$$G = \frac{D}{L}$$

$$G = \frac{24.35 \text{ ft} - 9.1 \text{ ft}}{200 \text{ ft}} \times 100$$

$$G = 7.62\%$$

2. Now find the distance between contours.

$$D = \frac{CI}{\%G} \times 100$$

$$D = \frac{2 \text{ ft}}{7.62 \text{ ft}} \times 100$$

$$D = 26.24 \text{ ft}$$

3. Starting at station $3 + 00$ and elevation 24.35 ft we must find the first even contour, the 24 contour.

$$TD = \frac{X}{CI} \times D$$

$$TD = \frac{24.35 \text{ ft} - 24 \text{ ft}}{2 \text{ ft}} \times 26.24 \text{ ft}$$

$$TD = 4.6 \text{ ft}$$

We can now step off the distance between contours 26.24 ft from contour 24.

4. Establish crown, given at 6 in.

$$\text{Crown} = 6 \text{ in.}$$

We must now find the travel distance for the crown.

$$TD = \frac{X}{CI} \times D$$

$$TD = \frac{6 \text{ in.}}{24 \text{ in.}} \times 26.24 \text{ ft}$$

$$TD = 6.55 \text{ ft}$$

5. Establish curb, given at 6 in.

$$\text{Curb} = 6 \text{ in.}$$

Find the travel distance for the curb and set it on the plan.

$$TD = \frac{X}{CI} \times D$$

$$TD = \frac{6 \text{ in.}}{24 \text{ in.}} \times 26.24 \text{ ft}$$

$$TD = 6.55 \text{ ft}$$

6. Draw the walk on the plan. The cross slope or pitch is given as ¼ in. per 6 ft.

$$\text{Walk} = 1\frac{1}{2} \text{ in.}$$

We must now find the travel distance for the walk and set it on the plan.

$$TD = \frac{X}{CI} \times D$$

$$TD = \frac{1.5 \text{ in.}}{24 \text{ in.}} \times 26.24 \text{ ft}$$

$$TD = 1.64 \text{ ft}$$

7. Establish 3:1 side slopes and blend new contours into the existing grade. (See Fig. 6-33.)

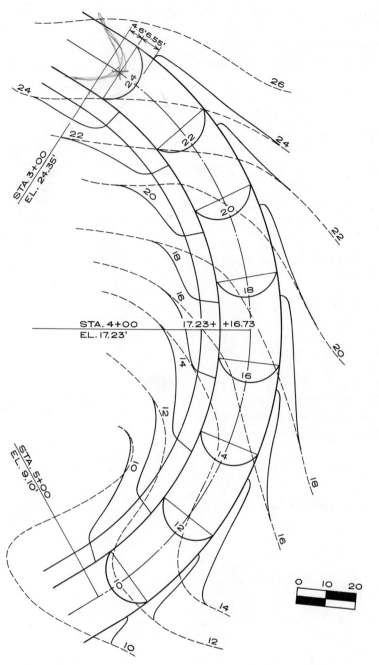

FIG. 6-33. Contours on roads.

EARTHWORK CALCULATION

Two types of grading which reshape existing contours are rough grading (before construction) and finished grading (after construction). Before rough grading is begun existing topsoil should be stripped from the area to be graded and stockpiled away from the construction area. Topsoil of good quality can be reused in the process of finished grading. Consider the kind of soil, how it reacts in cut and fill situations, and its bearing capacity. Allow approximately 10% for loss in weight and volume in moving soil and from shrinkage by spillage or excessive compaction. To determine amount of cut or fill we use the following methods.

Computing Cut and Fill by Borrow-Pit Method

To compute excavation of material for a rectangular building, see the following example and Fig. 6-34. A 10 × 20 ft rectangular excavation. Bottom of excavation is 95.3 ft.

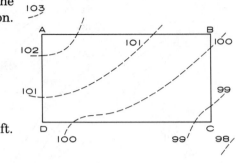

A	B	C	D
102.5 ft.	100.2 ft.	98.8 ft.	100.4 ft.
−95.3 ft.	−95.3 ft.	−95.3 ft.	−95.3 ft.
7.2 ft. +	4.9 ft. +	3.5 ft. +	5.1 ft. = 20.7 ft.

$$\text{Avg. ht.} = \frac{20.7 \text{ ft.}}{4} = 5.2 \text{ ft.}$$

FIG. 6-34. Excavation: cut and fill.

Volume = Average height multiplied by the area of the excavation and divided by 27 to arrive at cubic yards.

$$V = \frac{5.2 \text{ ft} \times 10 \text{ ft} \times 20 \text{ ft}}{27} = 38.5 \text{ cu yd}$$

When building excavations are more extensive, calculate the volume in the following manner.

1. Area is divided into a grid of squares of any convenient size.
2. Letter a corners which occur on one square, b corners common to two squares, c corners common to three squares, d corners common to four squares.
   all a's, b's, c's, and d's. (See Fig. 6-35.)
   all a's, b's, c's, and c's. (See Fig. 6-35.)
3. Compute the heights of corners of excavation and the sum of heights of all a's, b's, c's, and d's. (See Fig. 6-35.)

Bottom of excavation = 95.0 ft.

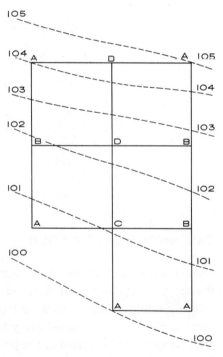

a's:

104.0 ft	105.0 ft	100.6 ft	100.0 ft	100.4 ft
−95.0 ft	−95.0 ft	−95.0 ft	−95.0 ft	−95.0 ft
9.0 ft +	10.0 ft +	5.6 ft +	5.0 ft +	5.4 ft = 35 ft

b's:

104.5 ft	101.8 ft	102.6 ft	101.5 ft
−95.0 ft "	−95.0 ft	−95.0 ft	−95.0 ft
9.5 ft +	6.8 ft +	7.6 ft +	6.5 ft sum of b's = 30.4 ft

c's: 101.1 ft
−95.0 ft
6.1 ft   sum of c's = 6.1 ft

d's: 102.2 ft
−95.0 ft
7.2 ft   sum of d's = 7.2 ft

$$\text{Volume} = \frac{\text{area of 1 square}}{27} \times \frac{\text{sum } a\text{'s} + 2 \text{ sum } b\text{'s} + 3 \text{ sum } c\text{'s} + 4 \text{ sum } d\text{'s}}{4}$$

FIG. 6-35. Extensive excavation problem: cut and fill.

$$\text{Volume} = \frac{20 \times 20}{27} \times \frac{35.0 + 2(30.4) + 3(6.1) + 4(7.2)}{4}$$

Volume = 529.3 cu yd

Average End Area Formula. Where cross sections occur through longitudinal cuts and fills, the average end area method is used to compute volume. The volumes obtained are not exact and tend to be in excess; however, since this formula is easily computed, it is often used. (See Fig. 6-36.)

$$V = L\,\frac{(A_1 + A_2)}{2} = \text{ft}^3 \text{ divided by } 27 = \text{yd}^3$$

V = Volume
A_1 and A_2 = Areas of two parallel faces
L = Horizontal distance between cross sections

Prismoidal Formula. The prismoidal formula is used for computations of volume where accuracy is required and the geometric solid is a prismoid (a solid with parallel but unequal bases with its other faces quadrilaterals or triangles).

$$V = \frac{L\,(A_1 + 4A_m + A_2)}{6}$$

V = Volume
A_1 and A_2 = Areas of successive cross sections or parallel faces
A_m = Area of section midway between A_1 and A_2
L = Horizontal distance between A_1 and A_2

Planimeter. A planimeter measures irregular areas. It converts the answer to square inches on a drum and disc while a tracing point is moved over the outline of the area to be measured. This instrument consists of two metal arms joined by a ball and socket joint. The pole arm is weighted and has an anchor point; the tracer arm has a tracer point, finger grip, recording wheel, and measuring scale. The measuring scales are usually calibrated to read in square inches to the nearest 1/100 of a square inch. (See Fig. 6-37.)

The anchor point is set at a spot outside the area to be measured. See if the arm will cover the whole area or if the anchor point must be changed. The tracer point is now set over the starting point, the vernier set to zero, and the tracing point moved clockwise around the area to be measured until it arrives at the starting point. A reading is now taken on the vernier. Enter four figures to eliminate possible errors in placing the decimal point. Now retrace the outline a second time and record a second reading which should be approximately twice the first. Divide the second reading by two and obtain the average of both readings. They should be within 1% of each other. If the instrument is carefully used, there should be no error greater than ½ to 1%.

Be careful to protect the instrument from bumps. Do not rub fingers over the recording wheel. Keep the instrument clean.

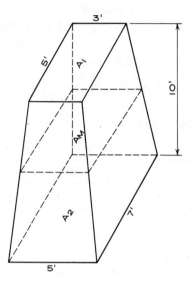

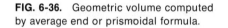

FIG. 6-36. Geometric volume computed by average end or prismoidal formula.

FIG. 6-37. Planimeter.

Example. 1.25 sq in. was the reading on the planimeter. 1 in. = 50 ft is the scale of the drawing. To find the volume we use the formula $V = L \times W \times H$.

$$1.25 \times 50^2 = 3125 \text{ sq ft}$$

$V = 3125$ sq ft $\times 2$ ft (height varies; it is the contour interval in this example)

$$V = 6250 \text{ cu ft}$$

$$V = \frac{6250 \text{ cu ft}}{27 \quad \text{cu ft/cu yd}} = 231.5 \text{ cu yd}$$

(See Table 6-1.)

Table 6-1. Sample Cut and Fill Planimeter Chart with Cut and Fill Computations[1]

Station	Cut 1st	Cut 2nd	Cut Cor.	Fill 1st	Fill 2nd	Fill Cor.	Area Cut	Area Fill	Length C/F	Volume Cut	Volume Fill
0 + 00							—	—			
0 + 50				1.15	2.30	1.15	—	46.00	0/50		1150
1 + 00				0.74	1.47	0.74	—	29.60	0/50		1890
1 ᛁ 50	0.45	0.92	.46	0.13	0.27	0.14	18.40	5.60	25/50	230	880
2 + 00	1.32	2.68	1.34				53.60	—	50/13	3600	36.4
2 + 50	1.02	2.04	1.02				40.80	—	50/ 0	2360	
3 + 00				.99	1.99	1.00	—	40.00	20/30	408	600
3 + 50				2.14	4.26	2.13	—	85.20	0/30		1878
4 + 00				1.87	3.74	1.87	—	74.80	0/50		4000
4 + 50				1.12	2.23	1.12	—	44.80	0/50		2990
5 + 00	0.03	0.06	0.03	0.13	0.13	0.13	1.20	5.20	5/50	3	1250
5 + 50	0.46	0.90	0.45				18.00	—	50/ 7	480	18.2
6 + 00	1.55	3.11	1.56				62.40	—	50/ 0	2010	
6 + 50	2.47	4.93	2.47				98.80	—	50/ 0	4030	
7 + 00	1.37	2.76	1.38				55.20	—	50/ 0	3850	
7 + 50	0.09	0.16	0.08	0.10	0.10	0.10	1.60	4.00	50/ 3	1420	6
8 + 00				2.08	4.15	2.08	—	83.20	2/50	1.6	2180
8 + 50				0.94	1.88	0.94	—	37.60	0/50	120	3020
9 + 00	0.23	0.47	0.24	0.02	0.04	0.02	9.60	0.80	25/50	1000	960
9 + 50	0.75	1.51	0.76				30.40	—	50/22		0.8

[1]See road alignment, p. 130.

Horizontal scale of sections   1 in. = 10 ft
Vertical scale of sections   ¼ in. = 1 ft
One square inch on planimeter   = 40 ft²

$$V = \frac{L (A_1 + A_2)}{2} = \text{ft}^3 \text{ divided by } 27 = \text{yd}^3$$

Total cut = 19,512.6 ft³ = 722.9 yd³
Total fill = 20,859.4 ft³ = 772.6 yd³

The figures in Table 6-1 were computed by first taking two consecutive planimeter readings to arrive at the readings for each cut or fill area. The two readings were then averaged and the corrected figure used in computing areas of cut or fill. One square inch on the planimeter as previously shown from the horizontal and vertical scales of the sections was 40 ft²/1 in. Each corrected planimeter reading was multiplied times 40 ft²/1 in. to compute the areas. On station 0 + 50, for example, to find the area, 1.15 in. × 40 ft²/1 in. = 46.00 ft². To compute the volume, the formula $V = L \dfrac{(A_1 + A_2)}{2} = \text{ft}^3$ is used. The length of the cut or fill between sections was determined from the sections and profile $p(00)$ and figures are given in the chart. The volume of fill between stations 0 + 00 and $0 + 50 = L \dfrac{(A_1 + A_2)}{2} = 50' \dfrac{(0 + 46.00)}{2} = 1150 \text{ ft}^3$.

FIG. 7-1. The concept of positive drainage is used at Southern Illinois University to permit runoff water to be directed away from buildings and into catch basins.

7 Site Drainage

SITE DRAINAGE

Surface Drainage

Controlling storm water runoff is a major factor in preparing a grading plan. To prevent problems caused by erosion or flooding, the principle of positive drainage is used—that is, diverting storm water away from a building or area and carrying it away from a site in a storm drainage system. Spot elevations are set at critical points adjacent to a building to provide drainage. Advantageous points must be chosen for placement of catch basins, and their connection to existing drainage channels in the area or to an existing storm drainage line must be considered. (See Figs. 7-2 and 7-3.)

Surface drain lines are called storm sewers and are constructed with tight or closed joints. Surface drainage can be provided by adjusting ground slopes to allow for runoff of storm water and its interception at various intervals in catch basins. Drainage systems can be one of the higher cost items in site development and special assistance from an engineer may be required.

The design of a drainage system is based on the amount of rainfall to be carried away at a given time. Runoff is that portion of precipitation which finds its way into natural or artificial channels either as surface flow during the storm period or as subsurface flow after the storm has subsided. Runoff is determined by calculating the volume of water discharged from a given watershed area and is measured in cubic feet of discharge

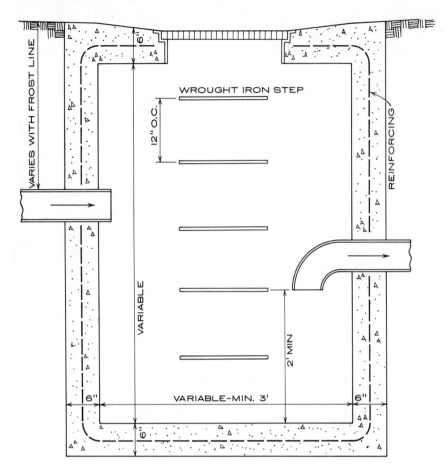

Labels in figure:
- VARIES WITH FROST LINE
- 6"
- WROUGHT IRON STEP
- 12" O.C.
- REINFORCING
- VARIABLE
- 2' MIN
- L
- 6"
- VARIABLE-MIN. 3'
- 6"
- 6"

FIG) 7-2. Catch basins intercept storm water and sediment is retained before water enters the outlet line of the drainage system. For this reason they must be cleaned periodically to prevent flooding.

per second. Runoff is affected by two factors: 1. intensity of a storm, amount of rainfall, and its duration; and 2. watershed characteristics— porosity of the soil, gradient or slope, and vegetative cover.

To calculate runoff, we use the rationale:

$$Q = CIA$$

Q = storm water runoff from an area, in cubic feet/second.
C = coefficient of runoff (percentage of rainfall that runs off).
I = intensity of rainfall in inches per hour for a particular locality.
A = area in acres.

In the design of drainage or storm sewer systems, the value Q is the key to the sizing of pipe. The following sequence gives the sizes of pipes the site planner may use.

1. Determine the required capacity of the sewer pipe by computing runoff from different drainage areas by formula $Q = CIA$.
2. Select pipe sizes and slopes having adequate velocity for self cleansing, such as 2.5 ft/sec minimum velocity.
3. Rim and invert elevations for pipe line must be known to determine pipe slope.
4. Establish a minimum depth for pipe lines below frost level. Information given in the following problem allows the use of the formula $Q = CIA$. The problem is an example of the method used to compute storm water runoff in cu ft/sec so that pipe sizes may be determined from the Manning Formula Chart (Fig. 7-5) for pipe lines Nos. 1 through 5 in Fig. 7-4. The site is located in northeast Kansas. Runoff is from grass

areas, with intensity for a ten year storm. Pipe lines have a slope of 0.1%.

Pipe line No. 1—areas $A + B = 4$ acres

$$Q = CIA$$
$$Q = .35 \times 2.4 \times 4$$
$$Q = 3.36 \text{ cu ft/sec}$$

Using the Manning chart, 3.36 cu ft/sec @ pipe slope of 0.1% = 16 in. pipe.

Pipe line No. 2—area $C = 2$ acres

$$Q = CIA$$
$$Q = .35 \times 2.4 \times 2$$
$$Q = 1.68 \text{ cu ft/sec}$$

Pipe lines Nos. 1 + 2 = 5.04 cu ft/sec
Using chart, 5.04 cu ft/sec @ pipe slope of 0.1% = 20 in. pipe.

Pipe line No. 3—areas $E + D = 3$ acres

$$Q = CIA$$
$$Q = .35 \times 2.4 \times 3$$
$$Q = 2.52 \text{ cu ft/sec}$$

Using chart, 2.52 cu ft/sec @ pipe slope of 0.1% = 14 in. pipe.

Pipe line No. 4—picks up lines Nos. 1 + 2 + 3

$$Q = 7.56 \text{ cu ft/sec}$$

Using chart, 7.56 cu ft/sec @ pipe slope of 0.1% = 22 in. pipe.

Pipe line No. 5—picks up area F + lines No. 1 through 4

$$Q = CIA$$
$$Q = 0.35 \times 2.4 \times 1$$
$$Q = 0.84 \text{ cu ft/sec}$$

Pipe lines Nos. 1 through 5 = 8.40 cu ft/sec
Using chart, 8.40 cu ft/sec @ pipe slope of 0.1% = 24 in. pipe.

The maximum rainfall to be expected for an assumed frequency such as once in 2 years, 5 years, 10 years, or 25 years can be used. If, for instance, a storm sewer could take the worst rainfall intensity expected in a two year period with no more than temporary ponding between curbs, our system would be designed at that intensity. If, however, overflow or flooding would result, a rainfall frequency of 5 or 10 years may be justified. (See Figs. 7-6 to 7-9.)

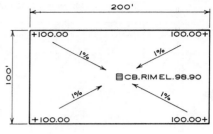

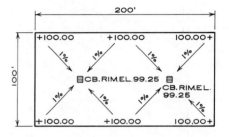

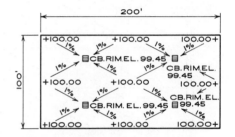

FIG. 7-3. Examples of catch basin locations on paved areas. Surface drainage influences design decisions in the initial layout of a project and is affected by type of surface material, soil, vegetation, size of area, and location of existing drainage channels or watershed areas. Excessive surface water must be removed by natural or constructed channels or carried away by subsurface pipe systems.

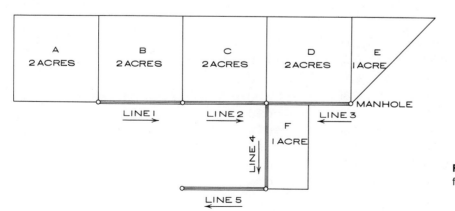

FIG. 7-4. Drainage areas and pipe lines for sample problems.

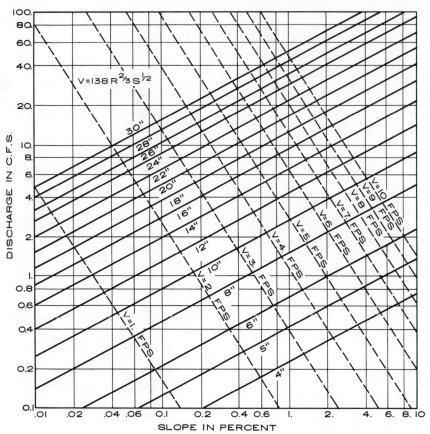

FIG. 7-5. Size of tile drain pipes. D. L. Yarnell, "The Flow of Water in Drain Tile," *U. S. Dept. Agr. Bull. 854*, 1920.

Values of C in Q = CIA

	Minimum	Optimum	Maximum
Roofs	0.90	0.95	1.00
Paving—concrete or asphalt	0.90	0.95	1.00
Macadam roads	0.70	0.80	0.90
Gravel	0.30	0.70	0.70
Unpaved streets	0.30	0.60	0.75
Cultivated land	0.30	0.60	0.82
Lawns or grass areas	0.10	0.35	0.60
Woodland	0.10	0.20	0.60
Pasture	0.10	0.16	0.60

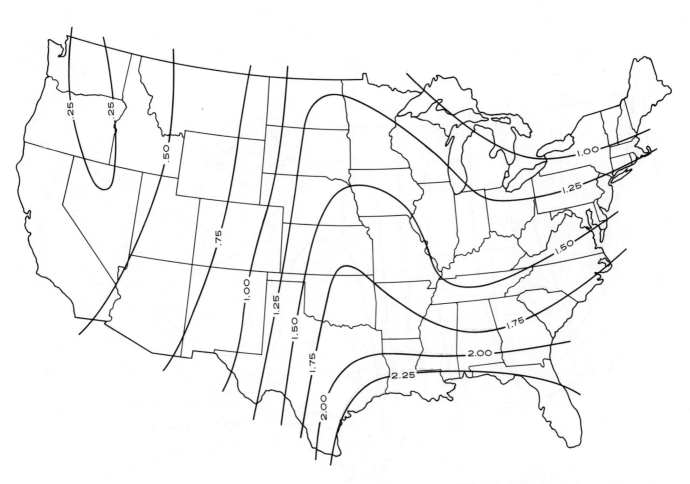

FIG. 7-6. Two-year storm: one hour rainfall in inches per hour. D. L. Yarnell, "Rainfall Intensity-Frequency Data," *U. S. Dept. Agr. Misc. Publ. 204,* 1935.

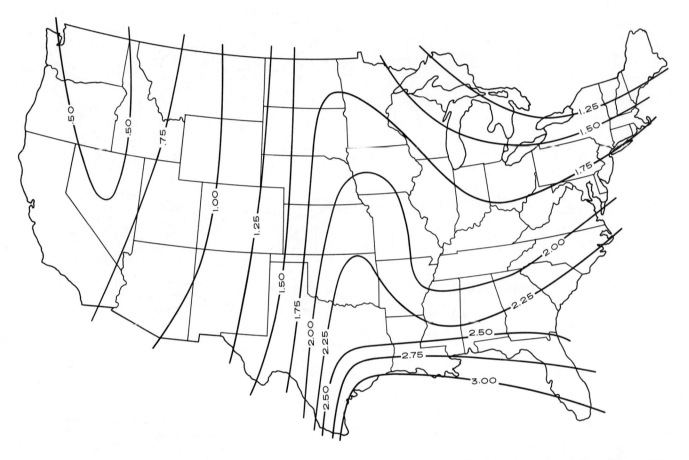

FIG. 7-7. Five-year storm: one hour rainfall in inches per hour. D. L. Yarnell, "Rainfall Intensity-Frequency Data," *U. S. Dept. Agr. Misc. Publ. 204,* 1935.

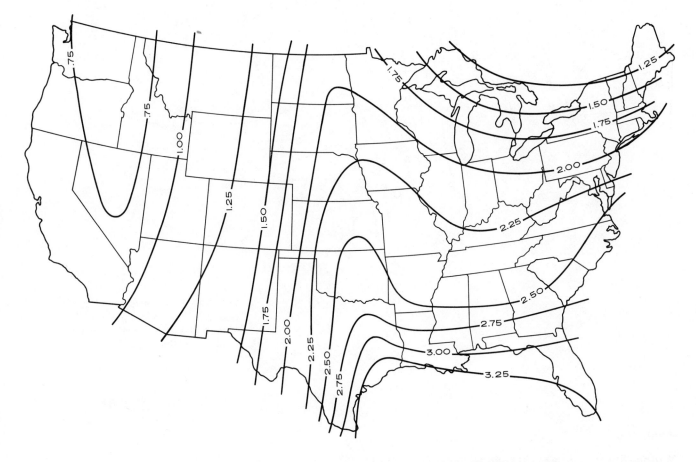

FIG. 7-8. Ten-year storm: one hour rainfall in inches per hour. D. L. Yarnell, "Rainfall Intensity-Frequency Data." *U. S. Dept. Agr. Misc. Publ. 204,* 1935.

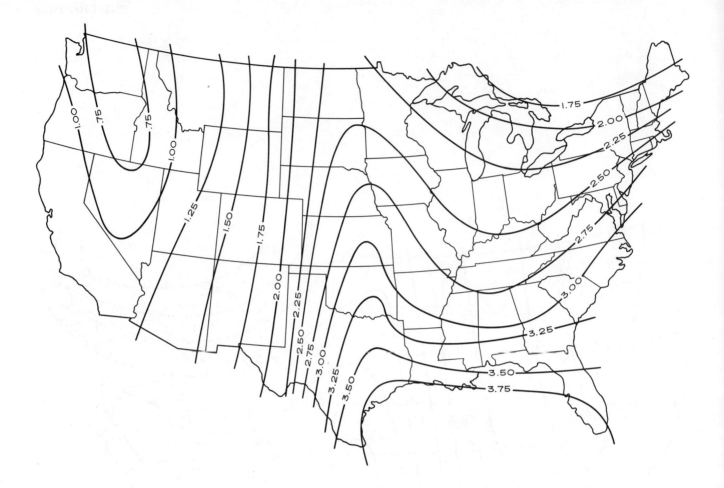

FIG. 7-9. Twenty-five year storm: one hour rainfall in inches per hour. D. L. Yarnell, "Rainfall Intensity-Frequency Data," *U. S. Dept. Agr. Misc. Publ. 204,* 1935.

Manholes

Manholes are used as a means of inspecting and cleaning sewer lines. They are placed at

1. Changes of direction of pipe lines.
2. Changes in pipe sizes.
3. Change in pipe slope.
4. Intersection of two or more pipe lines.
5. Intervals not greater than 300 to 500 ft.

Water causes scouring action when left uncontrolled. Drainage swales, usually under 10% grade, must be properly designed and stabilized to prevent erosion. The shape of the swale and its side slopes are vitally important. Velocity differs with the type of grass or other material used to line a swale. Minimum gradient for grass swales is 2%; the minimum for paved channels is 0.5 to 1%. To calculate the capacity of a channel, we must know the cross-sectional size, frictional factors, and volume and velocity of the water.

Subsurface Drainage

Subsurface drainage involves the control and removal of soil moisture. Subsurface drainage is concerned with

1. Carrying water away from impervious soils, clay, and rock.
2. Preventing seepage of water through foundation walls.
3. Lowering water tables for low flat land.
4. Preventing unstable subgrade or frost heaving.
5. Removing surface runoff in combination with underground drainage.

Subsurface drainage may be accomplished by providing a horizontal passage in the subsoil which collects gravitational water and carries it to outlets. Subsurface drain lines either have open joints or employ perforated pipe. Flow into subsurface drains is affected by soil permeability, depth of drain below soil surface, size and number of openings into the drain, drain spacing, and diameter.

Types of Systems

1. Natural: Used for areas that do not require complete drainage. (See Fig. 7-10.)
2. Herringbone: Used in areas of land with a concave surface with land sloping in either direction. This system should not have angles over 45°. (See Fig. 7-11.)
3. Gridiron: Used where laterals enter the main from one side. Mains and laterals may intersect at angles less than 90°. (See Fig. 7-12.)
4. Interceptor: Used near the upper edge of a wet area to drain such areas. (See Fig. 7-13.)

Outlets should discharge flow without erosion and prevent flooding when they are submerged. Tile lines should be placed 2½ to 5 ft below the soil surface. In moderately permeable soils a space approximately 24 ft wide should be employed for each foot of depth below soil surface. In general, depth varies with soil permeability.

The slope of tile may vary from a maximum of 2 to 3% for a main to a desirable minimum of .2% for laterals. A minimum velocity of 1.5 ft per sec is sometimes used. Drainage tile varies in size—4 in. is a minimum; 5 or 6 in. is used more frequently.

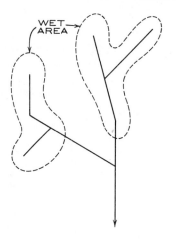

FIG. 7-10. Natural system.

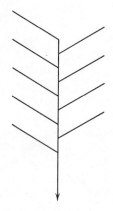

FIG. 7-11. Herringbone system.

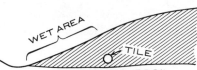

FIG. 7-12. Gridiron system.

FIG. 7-13. Interceptor system.

FIG. 8-1. Alignment of this residential entry drive is in complete contrast to the requirements of heavily traveled roads.

8 Alignment of Horizontal and Vertical Curves

ALIGNMENT

Although a straight line is the shortest distance between two points, it can be monotonous if aesthetic features are not considered. Road or walk alignment has two planes, horizontal and vertical. Curvature of this alignment gives the site planner an opportunity to fit a road to natural topography, while taking advantage of natural site features and keeping the road economically feasible. Good road design should attain a balance between curvature and grade to insure smooth flow of traffic, and so as not to mislead a driver by sudden variation in alignment or sight distance.

The center line of a road is used for reference to relate horizontal and vertical alignment and is measured in 50 ft intervals called stations. Center lines are comprised of tangents and straight lines joined by curves.

The following topics under alignment will present technical data for solving horizontal curves, vertical curves, and superelevation. A step by step outline procedure for laying out horizontal and vertical alignments in relation to each other is also presented. The calculations shown in this chapter involve the conventional methods generally used by site planners, especially in smaller offices; however, computers can be programmed to make these calculations and are often employed by engineers in designing major highways.

Horizontal Alignment and Computation

The following are three types of horizontal curves.

1. Arcs of a circle
   a. Simple curve: circular arc connecting tangents at each end. (See Fig. 8-2.)

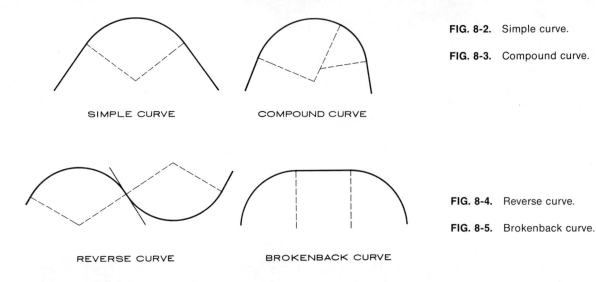

SIMPLE CURVE   COMPOUND CURVE

REVERSE CURVE   BROKENBACK CURVE

FIG. 8-2. Simple curve.

FIG. 8-3. Compound curve.

FIG. 8-4. Reverse curve.

FIG. 8-5. Brokenback curve.

b. Compound curve: two circular arcs of differing radii tangent to each other at the same side of a common tangent. (See Fig. 8-3.)

c. Reverse curve: curves on opposite sides of a common tangent. (See Fig. 8-4.)

d. Brokenback curve: short length of tangent connecting circular arcs with centers on the same side. (See Fig. 8-5.)

2. Arcs of spiral or easement curve: a curve of varying radius based on the cubic parabola, used at ends of circular curves and between segments of compound curves.

3. Parabolic arcs: arcs generally used for vertical curves.

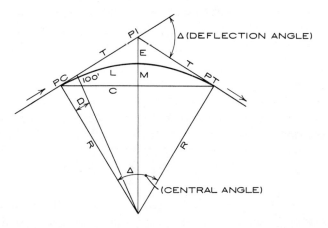

FIG. 8-6. Figure 8-6 presents functions of a simple curve.

PC = Point of curvature or beginning of curve.

PT = Point of trangency or end of curve.

PI = Point of intersection or intersection of two tangents.

Δ = Central or deflection angle.

T = Distance from PI to PC or PT.

R = Radius.

D = Degree of curve or angle at the center subtended by an arc of 100 ft.

L = Length of curve or arc length.

M = Middle ordinate or distance from center of curve to center of long chord.

C = Long chord or distance between PC and PT.

E = External distance or distance from PI to center of curve.

In drafting a road, sketch the center line of the road freehand, recognizing road design criteria. When the center line is established, redraft the road using tangents and curves calculated from the following formulas. (See Figs. 8-6 and 8-7.)

Measure Δ and T. Then calculate R.

$$R = \frac{T}{\tan \frac{1}{2}\Delta} \quad \text{or} \quad R = 5730$$

$$D = \frac{5730}{R} \qquad L = \frac{100\Delta}{D}$$

$$C = 2\,R \sin \frac{\Delta}{2}$$

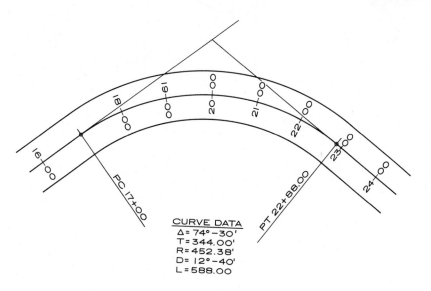

CURVE DATA
Δ = 74° – 30'
T = 344.00'
R = 452.38'
D = 12° – 40'
L = 588.00

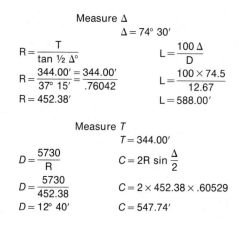

FIG. 8-7. Horizontal curve problem. Problem: Compute the following horizontal curve:

Measure Δ

Δ = 74° 30'

$$R = \frac{T}{\tan \frac{1}{2} \Delta°} \qquad L = \frac{100 \, \Delta}{D}$$

$$R = \frac{344.00'}{37° \, 15'} = \frac{344.00'}{.76042} \qquad L = \frac{100 \times 74.5}{12.67}$$

$$R = 452.38' \qquad L = 588.00'$$

Measure T

T = 344.00'

$$D = \frac{5730}{R} \qquad C = 2R \sin \frac{\Delta}{2}$$

$$D = \frac{5730}{452.38} \qquad C = 2 \times 452.38 \times .60529$$

$$D = 12° \, 40' \qquad C = 547.74'$$

Vertical Alignment Computations

In vertical alignment, two fixed points or grades must be assured to maintain existing road grades, grades of buildings, or other fixed conditions. The apex point of two grade tangents, therefore, is calculated.

From fixed apex A, a tangent line is projected to point D which is directly above fixed apex C. Grades of tangent lines AB and BC are set from study profiles, examples of which are shown further on in the text. We then calculate elevation of point D which is an extension of tangent line AB by multiplying % grade times horizontal distance and adding (or subtracting) to the elevation of apex A. Now calculate h, the vertical distance between D and C. Then determine the distance x where tangent lines A-D and B-C intersect.

$$x = \frac{h \, 100}{A}$$

x = horizontal distance from a given station to apex
h = vertical distance between two grades of given stations
A = algebraic difference

Calculate station of intersection point and its elevation; multiply % grade of BC by horizontal distance x and add (subtract) to elevation of apex C. (See Fig. 8-8.)

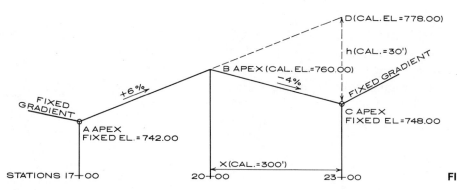

FIG. 8-8. Vertical alignment calculation.

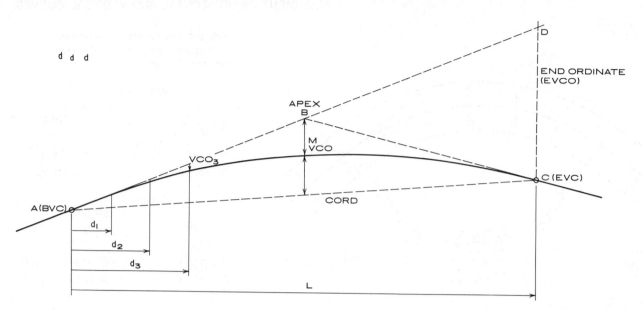

FIG. 8-9. Vertical curve functions.
BVC = Beginning of vertical curve
EVC = End of vertical curve
M = Middle ordinate
A = Algebraic difference—entering
grade minus leaving grade—
Eg.—(+6%) − (4%) = 10%
d = Horizontal distance of vertical
curve ordinate from BVC
EVCO = End VC ordinate at EVC
L = Length of VC
VCO = VC ordinate offset from tangent

$$VCORD = \frac{(d)^2\ EVCO}{L^2}$$

Vertical curves are parabolic rather than circular and are used for all changes of vertical alignment.

Mathematical Principles of a Parabola

1. Middle ordinate is bisected by the vertical curve.
2. Offsets from tangent lines vary as square of distance from point of tangent.
3. The second differences of the elevation of points at equal horizontal intervals are equal.

Figure 8-9 presents vertical curve functions. (See also Figs. 8-10 and 8-11.)

Superelevation

Superelevation compensates for centrifugal force. It reduces the danger of skidding on curves and induces traffic to keep toward the right side of the road.

Superelevation is accomplished by revolving the surface of the road about the center line as an axis. The amount of tilting depends upon the expected speed of the vehicle and radius of the curve. Full superelevation begins at the *PC* and continues the entire length of the curve to *PT*. The transition length required to acquire full superelevation is called runoff distance. The runoff distance is the same length back from the *PC* as from the *PT*. The transition from normal crowned section on a tangent to the fully superelevated section should be comfortable for safe operation of vehicles at highway design speed. There is no set method for this. Superelevation varies from ¼ to ¾ in per ft. A minimum effective rate is twice the crown.

Runoff distance is divided into three equal parts; the minimum distance used is 150 ft. (See Fig. 8-12.)

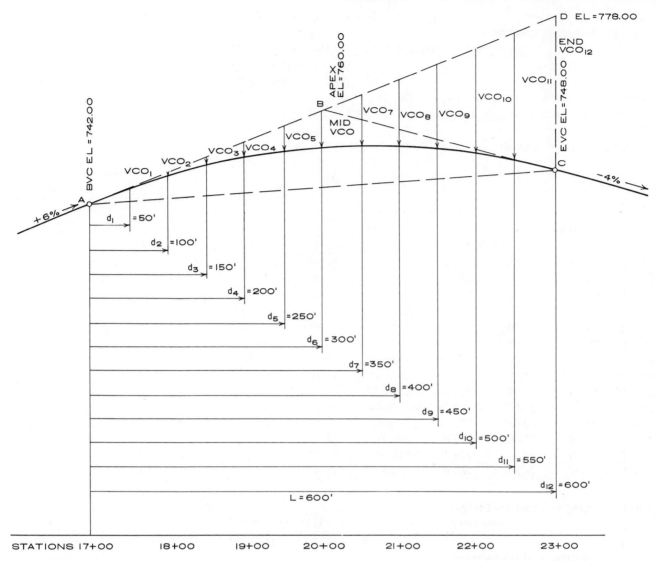

STATIONS 17+00   18+00   19+00   20+00   21+00   22+00   23+00

Formula for Superelevation

$$e + f = \frac{0.067\ V^2}{R} = \frac{V^2}{15R}$$

e = Superelevation in foot per foot of road width
V = Vehicle speed in mph
R = Radius of curve in feet
f = Side friction factor: 0.16 for 30mph and less, 0.15 for 40mph where
    e = max. of 0.08 ft/ft.
Rates on areas subject to snow and ice: 0.08 ft/ft.
Maximum for areas subject to snow and ice: 0.10 ft/ft. or where slow
    speeds are required on curves
Where traffic density and marginal development tend to reduce speeds:
    0.06 ft/ft. (See Fig. 8-13.)

General Procedure For Alignment Of Horizontal And Vertical Curves

1. Field reconnaissance of terrain for approximate location of road.
2. Preliminary topographic surveys are made if not already available.
3. List the design criteria for the road including speed, type, volume of

FIG. 8-10. Vertical curve problem. Compute the following curve: A +6% grade meets a −4% grade at station 20 + 00, elevation 760.00 ft. What are elevations at stations and half stations for the 600 ft. curve?

$$VCORD = \frac{(d)^2 \times EVCO}{L^2}$$

EVCO = "D" − "C"
EVCO = 778 − 748 = 30
Find VCO$_4$

$$VCO_4 = \frac{(d_4)^2 \times EVCO}{L^2}$$

$$VCO_4 = \frac{(200)^2 \times 30}{(600)^2}$$

VCO$_4$ = 3.33'
Find VCO − Middle ordinate

$$VCO = \frac{(d_6)^2 \times EVCO}{L^2}$$

$$VCO = \frac{(300)^2 \times 30}{(600)^2}$$

VCO = 7.5'

123

COMPUTE APEX STATIONS   20 + 00 ELEVATION <u>760.00'</u>

COMPUTE ALGEBRAIC DIFFERENCE

          +6% ENTERING GRADE − (−4% LEAVING GRADE) = 10%

COMPUTE <u>BVC</u> STATION   17 + 00 ELEVATION 742.00'

COMPUTE <u>EVC</u> STATION   23 + 00 ELEVATION 748.00'

COMPUTE ELEVATION OF ENTERING GRADE LINE AT <u>EVC</u> (<u>D</u>)   778.00'

COMPUTE END ORDINATE = $\dfrac{\text{ALGEBRAIC DIFFERENCE} \times \text{CURVE LENGTH}}{200}$ = 30.00'

COMPUTE MIDDLE ORDINATE = $\dfrac{\text{ALGEBRAIC DIFFERENCE} \times \text{CURVE LENGTH}}{800}$ = 7.5'

STATION	DISTANCE FROM <u>BVC</u>	TANGENT RISE OR DROP FROM <u>BVC</u> @ +6%	TANGENT GRADE ELEVATIONS	SQUARE OF DISTANCE FROM <u>BVC</u>	VC ORDINATES	VC ELEVATIONS
17 + 00	0.00'	0.00'	742.00'	0.00	0.00	742.00'
17 + 50	50.00'	3.00'	745.00'	2500.00	.20	744.80'
18 + 00	100.00'	6.00'	748.00'	10000.00	.83	747.17'
18 + 50	150.00'	9.00'	751.00'	22500.00	1.87	749.13'
19 + 00	200.00'	12.00'	754.00'	40000.00	3.33	750.67'
19 + 50	250.00'	15.00'	757.00'	62500.00	5.21	751.79'
20 + 00	300.00'	18.00'	760.00'	90000.00	7.50	752.50'
20 + 50	350.00'	21.00'	763.00'	122500.00	10.21	752.79'
21 + 00	400.00'	24.00'	766.00'	160000.00	13.33	752.67'
21 + 50	450.00'	27.00'	769.00'	202500.00	16.87	752.13'
22 + 00	500.00'	30.00'	772.00'	250000.00	20.83	751.17'
22 + 50	550.00'	33.00'	775.00'	302500.00	25.21	749.13'
23 + 00	600.00'	36.00'	778.00'	360000.00	30.00	748.00'
20 + 60_{HP}	360.00'	21.60'	763.60'	139600.00	11.63	751.97'

FORMULAS: TANGENT RISE OR DROP =

     VC ORDINATES = $\dfrac{\text{ALGEBRAIC DIFFERENCE } (\underline{\text{BVC}})^2}{2 \times \text{CURVE LENGTH}}$

<u>d</u> VALUES TIMES ENTERING

     HIGH OR LOW PT. = $\dfrac{\text{ENTERING GRADE} \times \text{CURVE LENGTH}}{\text{ALGEBRAIC DIFFERENCE}}$

GRADE %

VC ELEVATIONS (ADD OR SUBTRACT EACH <u>VC</u> ORDINATE TO TANGENT GRADE ELEVATIONS)

FIG. 8-11. Vertical curve data form.

traffic it can accommodate, number and width of lanes, and degree of curve permitted to carry out road design. (See Fig. 8-14.)

4. Using dividers, establish maximum desirable grade in order to study possible placement of road on steeper portions of topography. Paper locations should always be checked by field reconnaissance.

5. Draw a freehand line representing the center line of road trying various locations and taking existing site features into consideration. Start from an existing point of known elevation such as the center line of a road. (See Fig. 8-15.)

Horizontal Alignment Principles. Horizontal alignment must be as directional as possible with long flowing curves fitted to topography instead of long tangents which slash artificially across the land. Closely spaced short curves should be avoided along with brokenback

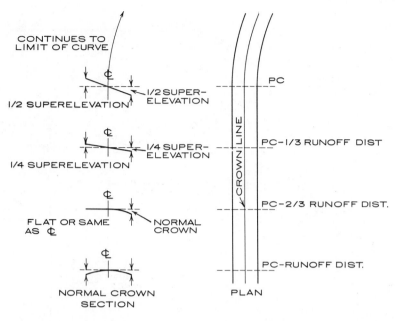

FIG. 8-12. Superelevation.

and reverse curves. The sharpest curves permitted by a design speed should only be used at critical locations. Strive for consistent alignment so as not to make a driver hesitate, for this causes accidents. Engineer the line by dividing the proposed alignment into tangents and arcs. Change for correction of degree of curve and use compound curves where necessary to achieve the nearest approach to the proposed alignment. Now redraw the more precise alignment. (See Fig. 8-15.)

6. Compute values for Δ, T, R, L, and C as shown on p. 120.
7. Check each curve by comparing the long chord distance C with its computed *PC-PT* value.
8. Carefully measure and label the stations along the center line of the road. Label *PC*, *PT*, *PCC* for compound curves.

RADIUS	DEGREE OF CURVE	30 MPH	40 MPH	50 MPH
5730	1	NC	RC	0.018
2865	2	0.016	0.025	0.035
1910	3	0.023	0.035	0.050
1432	4	0.029	0.044	0.062
1146	5	0.035	0.053	0.070
955	6	0.041	0.060	0.076
819	7	0.045	0.066	0.079
716	8	0.050	0.071	0.080 max
637	9	0.054	0.074	
573	10	0.058	0.077	
521	11	0.061	.079	
477	12	0.065	.080 max	
441	13	0.067	NC = Normal crown	
409	14	0.070	section	
358	16	0.074	RC = Remove adverse	
318	18	0.077	crown and super-	
286	20	0.079	elevate at normal	
260	22	0.080 max	crown slope	

[1]Elwyn E. Seelye, *Design: Data Book For Civil Engineers*, John Wiley and Sons, New York 1960.

FIG. 8-13. Superelevation for 30, 40, and 50 mph. where e max = 0.08.

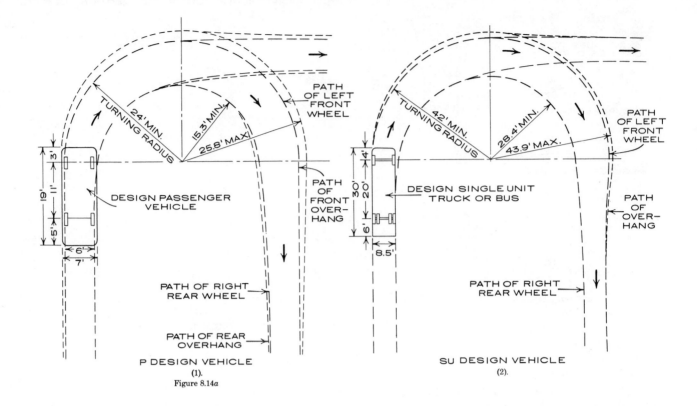

PATH OF LEFT FRONT WHEEL

TURNING RADIUS 24' MIN.

15.3' MIN.

25.8' MAX.

19' 11"

3'

5'

6'

7'

DESIGN PASSENGER VEHICLE

PATH OF FRONT OVER-HANG

PATH OF RIGHT REAR WHEEL

PATH OF REAR OVERHANG

P DESIGN VEHICLE
(1).

Figure 8.14a

PATH OF LEFT FRONT WHEEL

TURNING RADIUS 42' MIN.

28.4' MIN.

43.9' MAX.

30'

20'

4'

6'

8.5'

DESIGN SINGLE UNIT TRUCK OR BUS

PATH OF OVER-HANG

PATH OF RIGHT REAR WHEEL

SU DESIGN VEHICLE
(2).

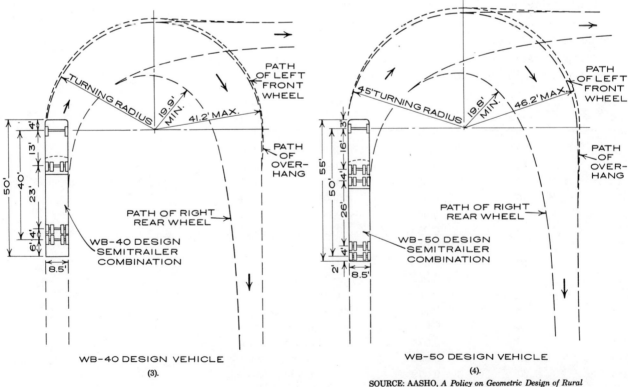

PATH OF LEFT FRONT WHEEL

TURNING RADIUS

19.9' MIN.

41.2' MAX.

50'

40'

13'

23'

4'

4'

6'

8.5'

WB-40 DESIGN SEMITRAILER COMBINATION

PATH OF OVER-HANG

PATH OF RIGHT REAR WHEEL

WB-40 DESIGN VEHICLE
(3).

PATH OF LEFT FRONT WHEEL

45' TURNING RADIUS

19.8' MIN.

46.2' MAX.

55'

50'

16'

26'

4'

4'

3'

2'

8.5'

WB-50 DESIGN SEMITRAILER COMBINATION

PATH OF OVER-HANG

PATH OF RIGHT REAR WHEEL

WB-50 DESIGN VEHICLE
(4).

SOURCE: AASHO, *A Policy on Geometric Design of Rural Highways*: 1965, AASHO Offices, Washington, D. C., 1966.

FIG. 8-14. Freehand road alignment.

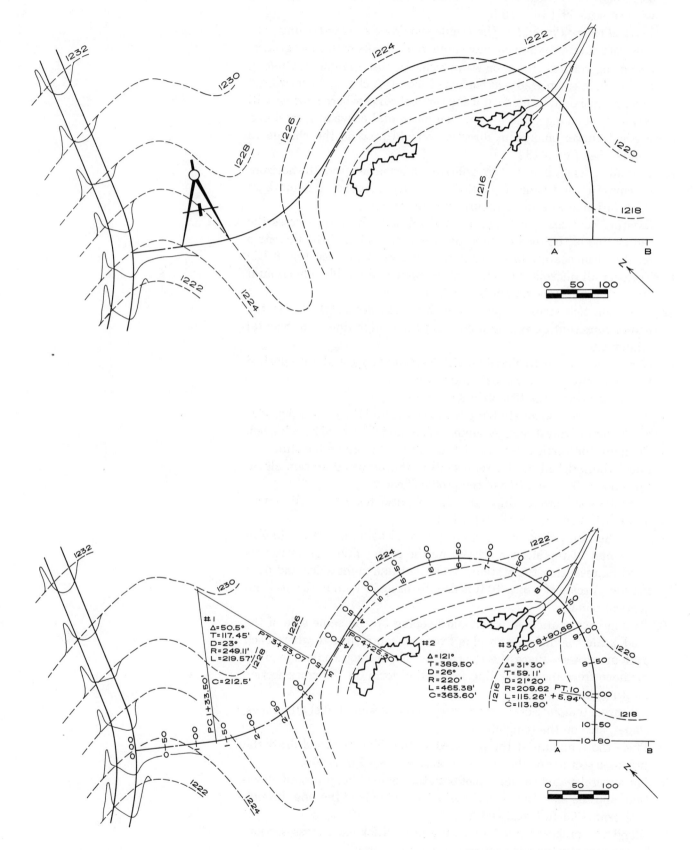

FIG. 8-15. Engineered alignment.

9. *Profile.* Draw a tentative profile, using it to adjust cut and fill and to set grades of vertical curves. A profile usually has an exaggerated vertical scale of 1 in. = 10 ft.

   Vertical Curve Principles. The profile should be smooth flowing with long vertical curves and not have numerous breaks with short grades. Avoid sag vertical curves on straight horizontal alignment. On long grades place steep grades at bottom of ascent. A change in horizontal alignment should be made at a sag vertical curve where a driver will be aware of change, and if there is a horizontal curve at a crest of a vertical curve, change in direction should precede the change in profile. (See Fig. 8-16.)

10. A profile is plotted by first transferring information from the horizontal curve to the profile. To do this a tick strip is prepared to mark off the relation of existing contours and stationing.

    Existing contours are ticked off and labeled where they cross the center line of the road by superimposing stationing of the tick strip on the road nearest to the contour being marked. (See Fig. 8-17.)

11. Transfer all information to the datum plane and establish horizontal stations and vertical axis as in Fig. 8-18.

12. Place the tick strip on the profile sheet and accurately locate the points representing contours crossing the center line of horizontal alignment.

13. Connect the points freehand or with a straight edge and use a dashed line since this represents existing topography.

14. Roll up and save the tick strip for further use.

15. Triangles are good for studying trial grades, and the proposed grades can be tentatively drawn. A balance of cut and fill should be achieved.

16. Compute the vertical curves; plot and draw the profile hardline.

17. Label the finished grades representing the proposed station elevations on each station line of the profile sheet.

18. Beneath each profile draw the diagramatic horizontal alignment and label. (See Figs. 8-18 and 8-19.)

19. *Cross Sections.* Cross sections are prepared using a vertical line in the center of the sheet representing the center line and horizontal lines representing the stations. Label left and right sides and each station. A scale of 1 in. = 10 ft is usually used for both horizontal and vertical planes.

20. Taking each station in order and keeping on the same side of the road, scale the distance on plan from the center line to where each contour crosses. Place the information about each contour and its distance from the center line in fraction form on the cross section plotting sheet.

21. Prepare a template of the road cross section design. Label all pitches, slopes, etc., on the template.

22. Place the template at the proposed station elevation and draw the proposed sections on the cross section sheet. (See Fig. 8-20.)

23. For superelevated sections, plot both the center line, proposed elevation, and the elevation of the road edge and extend the line through both points for full road width.

24. Blend the proposed line to existing ground for each cross section.

25. Check cross sections for agreement with the profile.

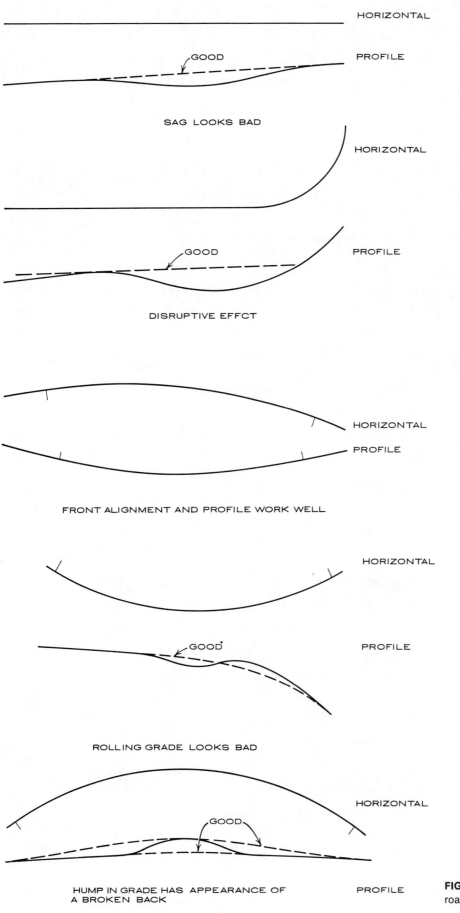

HORIZONTAL

PROFILE

GOOD

SAG LOOKS BAD

HORIZONTAL

PROFILE

GOOD

DISRUPTIVE EFFCT

HORIZONTAL

PROFILE

FRONT ALIGNMENT AND PROFILE WORK WELL

HORIZONTAL

PROFILE

GOOD

ROLLING GRADE LOOKS BAD

HORIZONTAL

GOOD

HUMP IN GRADE HAS APPEARANCE OF
A BROKEN BACK

PROFILE

FIG. 8-16. Examples of good and bad
road alignment.

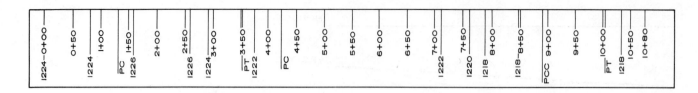

FIG. 8-17. Sample tick strip.

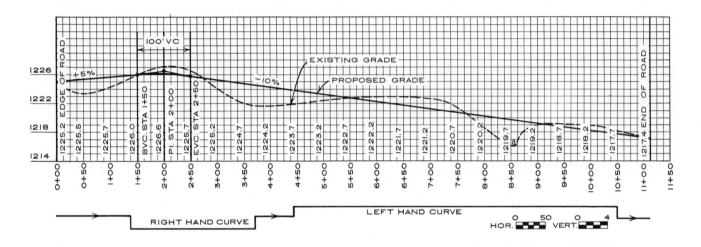

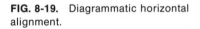

FIG. 8-18. Profile.

FIG. 8-19. Diagrammatic horizontal alignment.

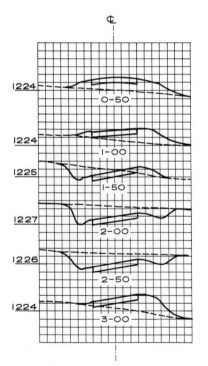

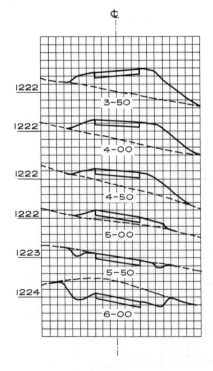

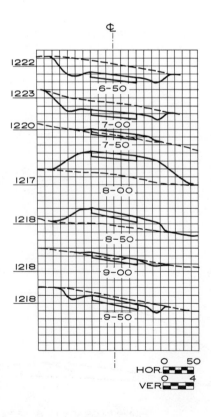

FIG. 8-20. Cross sections.

26. *Adjustment of Contours.* Going back to the plan draw the edges of the road, shoulder, and ditches.

27. Plot the proposed center line crossing of each contour on the plan by using the tick strip again and marking these first on the tick strip and then on the plan.

28. Compute the travel distance for crown, superelevation, shoulder, and ditch for each per cent of grade (00).

29. Draw in proposed contours in accordance with travel distance computations.

30. Make necessary blends with existing contours. Where possible use sections to determine location of the contour along the section of a station. (See Fig. 8-21.)

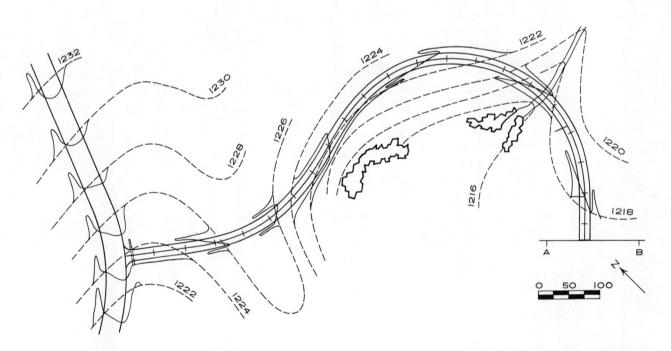

FIG. 8-21. Contours on the road.

FIG. 9-1. The concept of the natural landscape meeting a man-made stone podium is illustrated at Brandeis University, Waltham, Mass.

9 Details in the Landscape

To be carried to completion, successful design depends upon good detailing and supervision. Lack of good detailing may turn an otherwise good design into a mediocre-looking project. The site planner must see not only that details are well designed, but also that they are properly built during the construction phase.

Through photographic illustrations this chapter shows examples of details from many site planning projects including campus planning, urban plazas, shopping centers, parks, housing, civic centers, and office building complexes. Appropriate proportion, texture, and color are essential in the design of these details. Materials must be chosen in relation to each other and must be thought of in the context of the total design concept of a project.

Paving Materials

Paving materials were originally used to eliminate hazards from mud and dust and to form a smooth surface for ease of circulation. They are available today in a wide variety of textures and colors.

Stone. Stone, one of the oldest paving materials, offers a durable, long-wearing surface with a minimum of maintenance. Rubble and ashlar masonry are the two forms of stone used for paving. Rubble masonry is rough stone as it comes from the quarry but may be trimmed somewhat where necessary. Ashlar masonry is hewed or cut stone from the quarry and is used much more often than rubble for the surfacing of walks. (See Figs. 9-2 to 9-7.)

Brick. Brick is the oldest artificial building material in use today. It offers a great variety of textures and colors as well as flexibility in its use. Composed of hardburned clays and shales, brick is available in many colors due to variation in the chemical content of clay.

Three processes of making bricks are the sand-struck, wire-cut, and dry-press methods. The dry-press method forms bricks under high pressure and gives them a smooth surface with true edges and corners. Because they have a hard surface and resistance to wear and cracking, these bricks are best for outdoor paving.

Brick sizes follow:

Standard	$2\frac{3}{8} \times 3\frac{3}{4} \times 8$ in.
Norman	$2\frac{1}{4} \times 3\frac{3}{4} \times 12$ in.
Roman	$1\frac{5}{8} \times 3\frac{3}{4} \times 12$ in.
Baby Roman	$1\frac{5}{8} \times 3\frac{3}{4} \times 8$ in.

Brick may be laid on sand bases or on concrete slabs. The most common patterns are running bond, herringbone, and basket weave. (See Figs. 9-8 to 9-10.)

Concrete. Because it may be poured in place, has variety in texture and color, and forms a durable walking surface, concrete has been used extensively as a paving material. It is a mineral aggregate bound together by a cementing material, generally portland cement.

Concrete mixtures vary depending on the ratio of cement to sand to gravel; a sample mixture is one part portland cement, two parts sand, and three parts gravel. Fine and coarse grained aggregates are used in the mixture for concrete. Fine aggregates or sand generally range up to $\frac{1}{8}$ in. in diameter, whereas coarse aggregate is over $\frac{1}{4}$ in. in diameter and consists of crushed stone, gravel, or other inert materials. The maximum size of aggregates used in reinforced concrete is $1\frac{1}{4}$ in.

Concrete lends itself to variations in finish and may be smooth or rough, with aggregates exposed when desired. (See Figs. 9-11 to 9-15.)

Asphalt. Asphalt does not have the variety of textures that concrete does, although it gives a softer walking surface. Asphalt is not as durable as concrete, but it is less expensive and is used extensively for walk systems on college campuses and in park and recreation areas as well as in the construction of roads. (See Fig. 9-16.)

FIG. 9-2. Irregular fitted flagstone is used at the Morris & Stiles Dormitories at Yale University. Flagstone is generally more than 2 in. thick and grouted with portland cement where an impervious surface is required.

FIG. 9-3. Granite sets with slots for trees are used to give textural variety at the Los Angeles Civic Center.

FIG. 9-4. Granite sets are used to form this curvilinear paving pattern at the New Town of Vallingby, Sweden.

FIG. 9-5. Cobblestones are used in this children's play area at the New Town of Cumbernald, Scotland.

FIG. 9-6. Pebbles can be laid in concrete where an interesting texture is desired. Walking on this surface will be discouraged when the pebbles are laid on edge but encouraged when the pebbles are laid flat.

FIG. 9-7. A radial paving pattern is used in conjunction with the fountain at Lincoln Center, New York City.

FIG. 9-8. Brick pavers used in a fan pattern.

FIG. 9-9. Brick pavers used in a herringbone pattern.

FIG. 9-10. Brick bands with aggregate concrete infill at Skidmore College, Saratoga Springs, N. Y.

FIG. 9-11. The paving pattern of smooth concrete bands with aggregate concrete infill acts as an integral part of the design of the student union at Massachusetts Institute of Technology, Cambridge.

FIG. 9-12. The texture of smooth concrete blocks adjacent to aggregate concrete provides an interesting rhythm.

FIG. 9-13. There is contrast in color and size of rectangles in this paving pattern at Equitable Plaza, Pittsburgh.

FIG. 9-14. Varying colors of aggregate are used in this triangular paving pattern at Mellon Square, Pittsburgh.

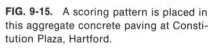
FIG. 9-15. A scoring pattern is placed in this aggregate concrete paving at Constitution Plaza, Hartford.

FIG. 9-16. Hexagonal pavers are used for pedestrian walks or plaza areas.

FIG. 9-17. Precast concrete grates allow water to be absorbed by trees and provide added interest in the paving pattern.

Paving and Drainage

When paving and drainage structures are well integrated, a utilitarian element may become visually pleasing. (See Figs. 9-17 to 9-19.)

Walls

Walls may be used to provide enclosure, articulate a space, or act as retaining elements. Brick, stone, and concrete are the materials most commonly used. The height and type of wall varies with its use in the over-all design concept of a project. They may be at seating height or may be up to 6 ft or more in height to provide privacy.

Used most extensively in high density projects where land is expensive, retaining walls may save usable areas that would otherwise be occupied

FIG. 9-18. Precast concrete drain.

Fig. 9-19. Drain used in conjunction with paving pattern.

FIG. 9-20. This brick retaining wall steps up the sloping site at Wellesley College, Wellesley, Mass.

FIG. 9-21. Irregular fitted stone retaining wall.

by banks. Walls may also act to reinforce and strengthen the design concept for a site; for example, on a steep site, they may reinforce an architectural concept by stepping up sloping land in conjunction with a building, or they may penetrate into the landscape and act as directional elements guiding people to a building. Determining the necessity of walls is therefore a site design and/or grading problem. (See Fig. 9-20.)

Generally, reinforced concrete is the most economical material for constructing retaining walls; however, dry stone masonry may also be used where good quality stone is available. Dry stone walls generally have a maximum height of 3 to 5 ft and need not have a footing greater than 12 to 18 in. below finished grade. On the other hand, reinforced concrete walls have a footing that may vary from 30 to 36 in. below frost level. (See Figs. 9-21 to 9-26.)

FIG. 9-22. Rubble stone retaining wall.

FIG. 9-23. Stone wall with coping.

FIG. 9-24. Dry stone retaining wall.

FIG. 9-25. Dry stone retaining wall.

Steps

Steps act as a connection between levels where grades are excessive. They may also be used to give prominence to entry areas or areas containing features such as fountains or sculpture. Steps should be designed for comfort with a riser and tread ratio which best fits the slope, considering the use of the area. (See p. 52.) Steps should be built into the slope and have a foundation that goes below frost level. They are constructed of various materials such as concrete, brick, and stone, or a combination of these. (See Figs. 9-27 to 9-30.)

FIG. 9-26. This serpentine brick wall winds its way around existing trees to form an outdoor terrace at the Loeb Drama Center, Cambridge, Mass.

FIG. 9-27. The detail of these steps has a high degree of refinement because of choice of materials, reveals, and shadow patterns: The University of California, Los Angeles.

FIG. 9-28. These board finished concrete steps form an integral part of the architectural character of the University of Colorado, Boulder.

Sculpture

Sculpture sometimes acts as a focal point in courtyard or plaza areas. It may be created from natural or artificial materials, and a great variety of forms, colors, and textures are possible. Stone and wood are natural elements which may be employed. These elements may be used as sculpture or in the formation of sculpture. Placement in a space depends upon sunlight and shadow patterns which give the object interest during different times of the day and with proper lighting at night. It should also be located to take advantage of varying sight lines. (See Figs. 9-31 to 9-36.)

FIG. 9-29. Brick used in the design of steps gives a warmth not inherent in concrete.

FIG. 9-30. Step details.

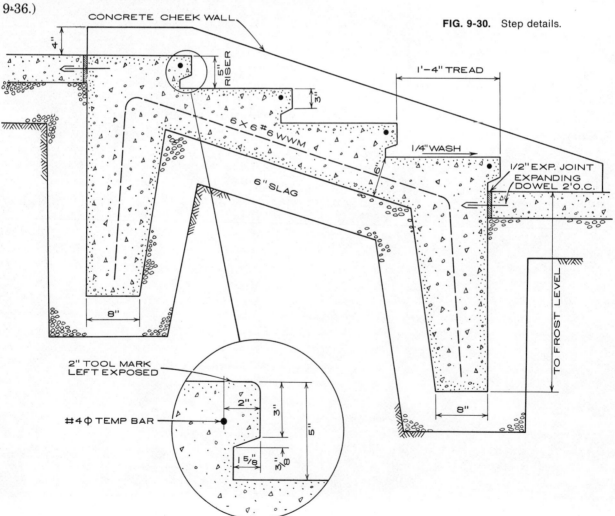

CONCRETE CHEEK WALL

4"

5" RISER

1'-4" TREAD

3"

6 X 6 #6 WWM

1/4" WASH

6" SLAG

1/2" EXP. JOINT
EXPANDING
DOWEL 2'0.C.

8"

TO FROST LEVEL

8"

2" TOOL MARK
LEFT EXPOSED

2"

3"

5"

#4 Φ TEMP BAR

1 5/8"

3/8"

FIG. 9-31. This sculptural bench acts as a focal point in a courtyard of the Connecticut General Insurance Company.

FIG. 9-32. Sculpture composed and oriented to be seen easily against a wooded backdrop of the Connecticut General Insurance Building.

FIG. 9-33. This sculpture takes advantage of sunlight and shadow patterns.

FIG. 9-34. Sculpture in conjunction with architectural elements at the University of California, Santa Cruz.

FIG. 9-35. A sculpture acts as the focal point for this space at Massachusetts Institute of Technology, Cambridge.

FIG. 9-36. Bronze sculpture at Expo 67.

Fountains and Pools

Water, a natural element, can be a prominent feature in the landscape. It may be used in fountains or pools for its reflective qualities, differences in sound, or cooling effect.

Programming the flow of water in fountains is accomplished by an electronic timing system which may control the night lighting sequence as well. These two systems should be coordinated to achieve maximum effect. (See Figs. 9-37 to 9-45.)

The sequence of programming of water in this fountain at the Los Angeles Civic Center is shown in Figs. 9-46 to 9-50. (See also Figs. 9-51 and 9-52.)

FIG. 9-37. This fountain integrates water with sculptural granite elements at Constitution Plaza, Hartford.

FIG. 9-38. Water flows out of a bowl in this fountain at the University of Colorado, Boulder.

FIG. 9-39. A seating area overlooks this fountain from which water gushes at the University of Colorado, Boulder.

FIG. 9-40. Water gushes in this fountain adjacent to the Travelers Insurance Building at Hartford.

FIG. 9-41. Water pours out of spouts in concrete elements at Northwest Plaza, St. Louis.

FIG. 9-42. At Northwest Plaza water also pours out of concrete elements that appear as abstract animals.

FIG. 9-43. The plaza area steps down to the fountain at Northwest Plaza, St. Louis.

FIG. 9-44. Water is used in conjunction with sculpture in this fountain at Northwest Plaza, St. Louis. Steps that lead to the fountain give it prominence and may be used for seating.

FIG. 9-45. Neptune Fountain at the Plaza, Kansas City, Mo.

FIG. 9-46. Los Angeles Civic Center.

FIG. 9-47. Los Angeles Civic Center.

FIG. 9-48. Los Angeles Civic Center.

FIG. 9-49. Los Angeles Civic Center.

FIG. 9-50. Los Angeles Civic Center.

FIG. 9-51. Water in a pool may be used for its reflective qualities.

FIG. 9-52. Gravel pool bottoms add interest in shallow water, but if the appearance of depth is desired, a pool bottom may be painted black.

Lighting

Outdoor lighting is used to illuminate pedestrian walkways, roads, and entry areas. It may also provide a dramatic effect when used in conjunction with reveals in walls to outline benches or other elements such as fountains. The level of illumination should vary with the intensity of use of areas. High intensity light is required for highways and other areas which are heavily used. Warmer colored illumination is best in quiet areas, along minor residential streets, and in parking areas. (See Figs. 9-53 to 9-60.)

FIG. 9-53. Outdoor lighting used in conjunction with the chapel at Massachusetts Institute of Technology, Cambridge.

FIG. 9-54. Lighting used on Constitution Plaza, Hartford.

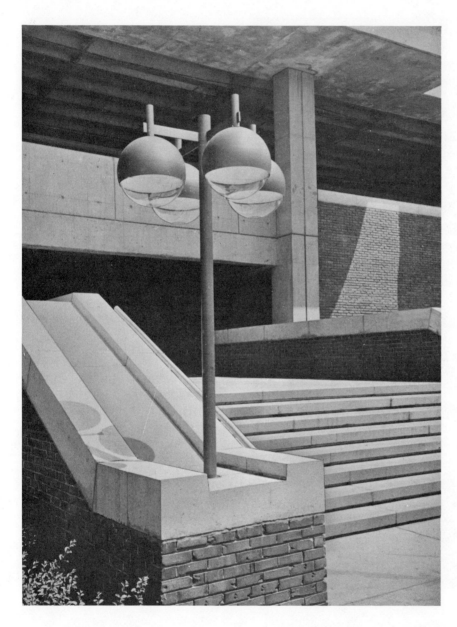

FIG. 9-55. Lighting used in conjunction with the entrance to Allegheny Center, Pittsburgh.

FIG. 9-56. Light used at Chatham Center, Pittsburgh.

FIG. 9-57. Lighting used at Expo 67.

FIG. 9-58. Light used to illuminate a roadway and walkway on either side of a dividing island at Gateway Center, Pittsburgh.

FIG. 9-59. Lights used near building entries at Southern Illinois University, Edwardsville.

FIG. 9-60. Lights used in conjunction with walls usually have metal covers so that they are not broken.

Benches

Benches have varying design but the two major types are those with or without backs. They are usually made of wood, concrete, or stone. Concrete or stone benches, particularly those without backs, may act as sculptural elements, are easily maintained, and less susceptible to vandalism. Wooden benches, especially those with backs, are most comfortable. Seating height above the ground should be 15 to 16 in. (See Figs. 9-61 to 9-69.)

FIG. 9-61. Wooden benches are used in a sitting area on Constitution Plaza, Hartford.

FIG. 9-62. Bench at the University of California, Santa Cruz.

FIG. 9-63. This wooden bench is supported by a steel frame at Northwest Plaza, St. Louis.

FIG. 9-64. This bench provides room for many people at the University of California, Los Angeles.

FIG. 9-65. Bench at Constitution Plaza, Hartford.

FIG. 9-66. Bench made out of a cut stone slab at Constitution Plaza.

FIG. 9-67. Seating used in a small courtyard.

167

Seating and Outdoor Lecture Areas

Outdoor lecture areas may act as the dominant feature of a space and provide varying amounts of seating. They may also act as theaters-in-the-round. (See Figs. 9-70 and 9-71.)

Seating in Conjunction with Raised Tree Planters

Seating is often combined with tree planters. The height of the planter depends on whether the tree is planted directly in the ground or on the top of a parking garage or other structure. (See Figs. 9-72 to 9-76.)

FIG. 9-68. This bench is made of cut stone supported by a steel frame at Skidmore College, Saratoga Springs, N. Y.

FIG. 9-69. This bench grows out of the paving at Southern Illinois University, Edwardsville.

FIG. 9-70. An outdoor lecture area to accommodate one class at San Mateo College, San Mateo, Calif.

FIG. 9-71. This outdoor lecture area can seat several hundred people at the University of Illinois, Chicago Campus.

FIG. 9-72. Seating and raised tree planter: University of California, Berkeley.

FIG. 9-73. Seating incorporated with planting as a design element: Busch Gardens, Sepulveda, California.

FIG. 9-74. Seating and raised tree planter in courtyard adjacent to Travelers Insurance Building, Hartford.

FIG. 9-75. Seating and raised tree planters set up a rhythm adjacent to Travelers Insurance Building, Hartford.

FIG. 9-76. Seating and raised tree planters become an integral design feature in this apartment complex plaza in Greenwich Village, N. Y.

Tree Planters and Pots

Tree planters must be of appropriate size to enable trees to grow above structures such as parking garages. Much better growth results where trees are planted directly in the ground. Pots are versatile and some may be moved or arranged for displays. A variety of materials may be used for their construction; concrete is the most common. (See Figs. 9-77 to 9-81.)

Plant Material

Plant material is important for its use as a design element. It may articulate space, provide privacy, or act as a focal point. It also may provide shade, act as a wind break or surfacing material, filter or enframe a view, and it has shadow patterns which add interest during daylight hours. (See Figs. 9-82 to 9-93.)

FIG. 9-77. These precast concrete planters are used above the parking garage at Constitution Plaza, Hartford.

171

FIG. 9-78. Pots must be large enough for the variety of flowers or plants grown in them.

FIG. 9-79. Tree planter and pots used in a small court.

FIG. 9-80. Flower pots used at Chatham Center, Pittsburgh.

FIG. 9-81. Flower pots used at Constitution Plaza, Hartford.

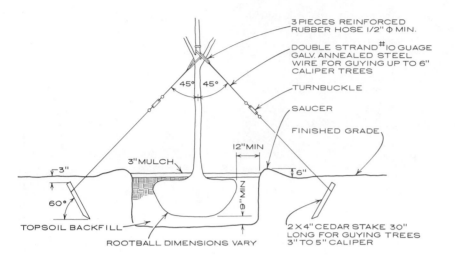

3 PIECES REINFORCED RUBBER HOSE 1/2" Φ MIN.

DOUBLE STRAND #10 GUAGE GALV. ANNEALED STEEL WIRE FOR GUYING UP TO 6" CALIPER TREES

TURNBUCKLE

SAUCER

FINISHED GRADE

45° 45°

12" MIN

3" MULCH

3"

6"

60°

9" MIN

TOPSOIL BACKFILL

ROOTBALL DIMENSIONS VARY

2 X 4" CEDAR STAKE 30" LONG FOR GUYING TREES 3" TO 5" CALIPER

FIG. 9-82. Tree planting detail.

FIG. 9-83. This hedgerow of trees was saved in the New Town of Cumbernald, Scotland.

174

FIG. 9-84. This bosk of trees gives shade to the seating area below in San Francisco.

FIG. 9-85. Trees may be used for their sculptural qualities.

FIG. 9-86. Trees are used for their shadow patterns.

FIG. 9-87. Refined planting complements this library at Harvard University.

FIG. 9-88. Trees used in the refinement of the landscape at John Deere, Moline, Ill.

FIG. 9-89. Trees used at the Morris and Stiles Dormitories, Yale University.

FIG. 9-90. Tree wells are used to save existing trees where the grade level changes more than 6 in. in cuts or 12 in. in fills: University of California, Santa Cruz.

FIG. 9-91. Groundcover may be used for ease of maintenance.

FIG. 9-92. Parking lots may be softened by the use of plant material. Here shrubs are used as groundcover.

FIG. 9-93. A moat filled with groundcover separates the building from the pedestrian walk system at Foothill College, Los Altos, Calif.

Bibliography

American Association of State Highway Officials. *A Policy on Geometric Design of Rural Highways: 1965* Washington, D. C.: A.A.S.H.O. General Offices, 1966.

Baker, Geoffrey, and Bruno Funaro. *Parking.* New York: Rheinhold, 1958.

Brinker, Russell C., and Warren C. Taylor. *Elementary Surveying.* 3d ed. rev. Scranton, Pa.: International Textbook, 1955.

Buckman, Harry O., and Nyle C. Brady. *The Nature and Property of Soils: A College Textbook of Edaphology.* 6th ed. rev. New York: Macmillan, 1960.

Church, Thomas D. *Gardens Are for People: How to Plan for Outdoor Living.* New York: Rheinhold, 1955.

Community Builders Council. *The Community Builders Handbook.* Executive ed. Washington, D. C.: Urban Land Institute, 1960.

Eckbo, Garrett. *Landscape for Living.* New York: F. W. Dodge Corp., 1950.

Eckbo, Garrett. *Urban Landscape Design.* New York: McGraw-Hill, 1964.

Frevert, Richard K. *et al. Soil and Water Conservation Engineering.* New York: Wiley, 1955.

Halprin, Lawrence. *Cities.* New York: Rheinhold, 1963.

Hubbard, Henry Vincent, and Theodora Kimball. *An Introduction to the Study of Landscape Design.* 2d ed. rev. Boston: Hubbard Educational Trust, 1929.

Kassler, Elizabeth B. *Modern Gardens and the Landscape.* New York: The Museum of Modern Art, 1964.

Lynch, Kevin. *Site Planning.* Cambridge, Mass.: The M. I. T. Press, 1962.

Meyer, Carl F. *Route Surveying.* 3d ed. rev. Scranton, Pa.: International Textbook, 1962.

Miller, E. Willard, and George T. Renner *et al. Global Geography.* 2d ed. rev. New York: Thomas Y. Crowell, 1957.

Olgay, Victor. *Design with Climate.* Princeton, N. J.: Princeton University Press, 1963.

Parker, Harry, and John W. MacGuire. *Simplified Site Engineering for Architects and Builders.* New York: Wiley, 1954.

Ramsey, Charles G., and Harold R. Sleeper. *Architectural Graphic Standards,* 5d ed. rev. New York: Wiley, 1956.

Seelye, Elwin E. *Data Book for Civil Engineers: Volume I, Design.* 3d ed. rev. New York: Wiley, 1960.

Simonds, John Ormsbee. *Landscape Architecture: The Shaping of Man's Natural Environment.* New York: F. W. Dodge Corp., 1961.

Wyman, Donald. *Shrubs and Vines for American Gardens.* New York: Macmillan, 1958.

Wyman, Donald. *Trees for American Gardens.* New York: Macmillan, 1959.

Illustration Credits

All drawings and photographs not otherwise credited were drawn or photographed by the author.

Pages

INDEX